MW00615471

EXTREME DAYS

A STRATEGY FOR AN AWAKENING ON YOUR CAMPUS

ADAPTED FROM:

AUTHOR | CO-AUTHOR
RICHARD MULL | **ANDREW MULL**

(COLLEGE EDITION)

Operation Light Force is an international Christian organization. It is our mission to grow biblical disciples, and to bring about in their lives personal and **global spiritual transformation.** We envision the transformation of an entire generation of believers who have grown to **think, act and be like Jesus –** for their entire lives.

Original copyright © 2003 by Richard Mull
Updated edition © 2015 by Richard & Andrew Mull

ISBN 978-0-9850132-1-9

Cover and Interior Design by Jeff Damm Design
Interior Layout by Jaydee Abraham (jaydee.abraham@yahoo.com)

Some of the anecdotal illustrations in this book are true accounts of actual events, and are included with the permission of the persons involved. All other illustrations are composites of real situations, and any resemblance to people living or dead is coincidental.

Unless otherwise identified, all Scripture quotations in this publication are taken from the HOLY BIBLE: NEW INTERNATIONAL VERSION® (NIV®). Copyright © 1973, 1978, 1984 by International Bible Society. Used by permission of Zondervan Publishing House. All rights reserved. Other versions used (and so noted) include: Contemporary English Version (CEV). © 1992 by American Bible Society and King James Version (KJV).

Mull, Richard, 1964-Present
Mull, Andrew, 1993-Present

OPERATION LIGHT FORCE
2310 Leonard Drive
Seffner, FL 33584
www.operationlightforce.com
www.40dayrevolution.com
813.657.6147 phone

PREFACE

Revolution!

The word revolution itself stands for radical change. Revolutions change lives. Revolutions change nations. Revolutions have changed history. Revolutions can change the future.

Revolutions are always preceded by a growing awareness that things are not the way they ought to be. It has become obvious that there is a great need for change on the campuses of America. Some feel that answers do not exist. But an answer does exist.

It Is Time for a Revolution!

Revolutions are not glamorous. They are not for the weak. Every revolution is the product of a generation whose motto is "No Fear." It is our challenge to **BE** such a generation

Our weapons are not guns, knives, or bombs, but rather something much more powerful. Campuses are being revolutionized through the power of God's love, as it is manifested through prayer, blessing, and serving others in the lives of a "Revival Generation."

When Babylon's laws conflicted with Daniel's faith, he chose, rather than to disobey God, to pray, and face the consequences.

Will you bring prayer back to your school? Will you be a part of The Revolution?

"—we must fight!—I repeat it, Sirs, we must fight!! "...They tell us, sirs, that we are weak—unable to cope with so formidable an adversary ...Sir we are not weak, if we make a proper use of those means which the God of nature hath placed in our power ...Besides, Sir, we shall not fight our battles alone. There is a God who presides over the destinies of nations and who will raise up friends to fight our battles for us. The battle, Sir, is not to the strong alone; it is to the vigilant, the active, the brave.

"...Gentlemen may cry, peace, peace—but there is no peace. The war is actually begun! Is life so dear or peace so sweet to be purchased at the price of chains and slavery? Forbid it, Almighty God!—I know not what course others may take; but as for me, ...give me liberty, or give me death!"

—PATRICK HENRY, LEADER IN THE AMERICAN REVOLUTION,
FROM "THE INEVITABLE WAR" SPEECH MARCH, 1775.

Our passion is to awaken believers to a desire to reach their cities and to help those who want to reach their cities become more effective in doing so. Many believers already have a passion to pray for and reach out to their neighbors, coworkers, and friends. We find that many believers want to care, they want to reach out, but they don't know how. Since God's Word is clear in calling us to show the world God's love, we believe God has called us to help equip believers to do that in an effective, practical and powerful way.

Since 1999 hundreds of thousands of believers have carried out different versions of "Extreme Days" and have seen God use them to transform their campuses, homes, schools and cities for Christ. Believers have reported incredible results not only in their personal lives, but also on their campuses, in their cities, workplaces, schools, and neighborhoods. For years, people have been asking help to bring transformation to their communities. This is why we created "Extreme Days."

These 40-Days are not what you might call typical. They are hardcore challenges that are specifically designed to take you to a new level in impacting your world with God's love through prayer, service, and blessing evangelism. The only way to bring about a revolution is to get radical.

Each day of the 40-Days you will get a mission. This is a practical assignment that you can carry out in only a few minutes during the week. It allows each person to get a hands-on sampling of the daily assignments included in "Extreme Days." Doing the assignments with a group will give you a sense of accomplishment which can motivate you and others to continue with the other assignments for the week.

Let us know how your revolution goes! E-mail us at operationlightforce@gmail.com.

Sincerely,

RICHARD & ANDREW MULL

Director, Operation Light Force, Inc.

[HOW TO USE THIS MANUAL?]

This is more than a book. This manual is a **40-day guide** to assist you in bringing spiritual transformation to the world around you. The following section of the book will explain 9 key aspects of bringing about spiritual transformation to the world around you. Read this section very carefully so that you will get a better understanding of the journey you are about to embark on.

I would caution you that this is not simply a 6-week journey. Once your 40 days are finished, if God answers our prayer, you will begin a lifetime of praying for, blessing, serving, and telling others about Jesus. One man at the end of the 40 days chastised us here at Operation Light Force because he felt that we had deceived him. We told him that the purpose was for God to work through him to transform others. In reality, he said, God had transformed him as much as God had transformed anyone around him.

I pray that God will indeed transform your life and through you spread the fragrant aroma of Christ. May God bring transformation through you to this world in desperate need of Jesus.

After you have read the 9 Keys to Transformation, you are ready for lesson 1 and the first week of the revolution. The book was designed to be used in a small group context and to follow the lesson outline from "Transformation Out of the Box." If you purchase the box to use on your own and are not watching the videos then the answers to the questions can be found in the back of the book.

[9 KEYS TO TRANSFORMATION]

WHAT IS TRANSFORMATION?

Do you know that God determined exactly where you would live and has a purpose for you to fulfill there? Do you realize that He placed you in your position where you work for a purpose?

When believers come to understand the purpose and call of God on their lives, a transformation begins to take place. The first thing to be transformed is their sense of purpose. When believers realize God has put them where they are in life for specific reasons and that God has a plan that only He can fulfill, it motivates those believers and fills their lives with purpose. The once mundane becomes meaningful.

You may say, "Prove it. Does God really care where I live?" Okay, that's easy. Let's look at what the Apostle Paul says in Acts 17:24-27.

> "The God who made the world and everything in it is the Lord of heaven and earth and does not live in temples built by hands. And He is not served by human hands, as if He needed anything, because He Himself gives all men life and breath and everything else. From one man He made every nation of men, that they should inhabit the whole earth; and He determined the times set for them and the exact places where they should live. God did this so that men would seek Him and perhaps reach out for Him and find Him, though He is not far from each one of us."

God determined the time of your birth and exactly where you would live. WHY? So that you could be a light to your neighbors, fellow students, co-workers, and others with whom you have regular contact. The passage clearly says that when people seek God, they can find Him.

Then it says, "Though He is not far from each one of us." Why would the passage make this distinction? Could it be that the ways that God is near us is that He has believers strategically in place to carry out His divine purpose of reconciling a lost world to Himself.

Much of our Christian activity has totally missed the mark of what Christ intended. Jesus chose 12 men and sent them out. We have spent most of our time, talent, and money on efforts trying to better the services within the church, and hoped and prayed that people would come in. When we realize that God is sending us out into our own neighborhood or on our campuses, then the church can begin to mobilize into effective ministry and see a city transformed. The following true story illustrates what happens when a Christian fulfills God's purpose.

Michele became a Christian and immediately wanted to go into ministry. She worked at a secular amusement park that had a brewery and she felt that this conflicted with her newfound faith. God began to work in Michele's heart and gave her a vision to bring her newfound faith into the workplace. She began to ask God to change the amusement park.

Michele arrived at work early every day and prayed in front of each of her manager's doors. Soon she began to invite people who knew how to pray effectively to walk around the park and pray. People all over the park began to come to know Jesus. Bible studies began to spring up and the spiritual climate of the entire park was transformed. I will explain more about fasting later in this chapter.

This story is one example of how becoming an agent of change in your world can make a powerful impact. God is calling all Christians to begin to see His purpose and vision for their lives and bring transformation to their city.

In Matthew 5:14-16 Jesus said, "You are the light of the world. A city on a hill cannot be hidden. Neither do people light a lamp and put it under a bowl. Instead, they put it on its stand, and it gives light to everyone in the house. In the same way, let your light shine before men, that they may see your good deeds and praise your Father in Heaven."

Many Christians think that letting their light shine means not to "drink, smoke, cuss or chew tobacco and especially don't go with girls that do." This viewpoint doesn't seem to be making a big difference, though, on the world around us.

Have you been a light to bring transformation in this dark world? Do you want to be? This book is a powerful tool to help you get started. The challenges it contains will help you develop a life-style that is geared toward making the maximum impact on the world within your living and educational environment. Most of the assignments can be done in less than 10 minutes. Some assignments will take thought and planning and a little more time. You will benefit and see transformation in direct proportion to your time spent in prayer, your level of commitment, and consistency, fasting, and carrying out the assignments.

Your 40-Day fast will be a critical element in the victory. Those of you already familiar with fasting may be ready for an all-out biblical fast. For many, fasting is a new and unsettling proposition. Don't get stressed about the fast. The main issue is setting aside 40 days to seek the Lord for a transformation in your life, your neighborhood, your campus, and your city. If all you can fast is peanut butter and that is a sacrifice for you, then fast peanut butter with all your heart as unto the Lord. You will see God do the miraculous according to the level of faith you show.

Before you read any further, ask yourself this, "Am I willing to follow Jesus?" He is calling you now, as He called the 12 disciples, "Come, follow Me, and I will make you fishers of men."

WHAT IS A LIGHTHOUSE PRAYER?

A **Lighthouse of Prayer** is a term to represent a believer consciously choosing to be a light to the world he lives in. To be a Lighthouse, a **believer** intentionally prays for, seeks to serve and bless his fellow students, dorm mates, and neighbors with the goal of showing the light of Christ to others. Your focus could be your dorm, home, apartment, campus, or workplace.

Most Christians want to be a light; they want to make a difference and be a light in this world. They just don't know how to, or have trouble making prayer and serving others a life-style.

This little book will help you become a light on your campus, your workplace, your neighborhood, and in every sphere of influence. What is meant by sphere of influence? A sphere of influence is anywhere that you find yourself on a regular basis and are able to make an impact. Your spheres of influence include your home, campus, workplace, gym, hair salon, church, and anywhere else you spend time and energy.

Simply knowing the concept of being a light often does not translate into practical behavior. This book will give you daily challenges that will help you establish a life-style of letting your light shine in this dark world. You will use the lighthouse classroom chart as a tool to help you practically apply these principles. You may want to draw a diagram of your campus to apply the same concepts. Every Sunday your assignments will focus on being a Lighthouse in your dorm or neighborhood.

Here is a sample "before" and "after" model of the format you will develop:

Don't worry if you haven't filled out the entire chart by the end of the 40-Days. Set a goal as to how much of your worksheet you will complete during the 40 days. Keep the chart in your Bible, on your desk, or on your refrigerator. Do not write sensitive things others do not need to see.

You can download this helpful chart online at *www.40-DayRevolution.com.*

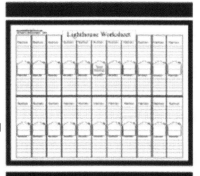

[UNITING FOR TRANSFORMATION]

" ... If as one people speaking the same language they have begun to do this then nothing they plan to do will be impossible for them." Genesis 11:6

God Himself said, "nothing would be impossible for them." What was the powerful key that God knew would give man more authority? Unity was the key. One people with one language, one goal, and one purpose could do the impossible. Reaching a campus, a city is impossible as long as there are Lone Ranger Christians and Lone Ranger Churches.

Carlos Anacondia, who in the revival of Argentina has seen over 1 million conversions, is quoted as saying that if there is 10% unity in the churches of a city, you will see 10% of the power of God; 30% unity will see 30% of the power of God. If you have 100% unity, you will have an open heaven . God has used him greatly in Argentina where cities have experienced church growth of 500% citywide.

George Otis Jr., in his video "Transformations," has given us tangible evidence of what a united church can see happen if the believers are united for the right purpose. If you have seen the video, you will notice that the elements of fasting, unity among churches, prayer, worship, and the power of God are all evident. Do you want to see your city transformed? Do you believe your city can be changed? If you keep doing what you have been doing, will your city be changed?

Some of you will get this book and not know anyone who has the faith to see the change on your campus. You need know that God has used many other individuals who gave themselves to Him to bring transformation to their campus and city. Will you be among those who believe and become an agent to transform your campus?

God may lead you to others who will lead many more to unite for the transformation of your campus. Everyone needs to find others to unite with him/her. Whether there are two, 10,000, or 1,000,000 realize that there is more power when believers unite.

For too long we have focused on coming together for large events. If God's children are going to transform this world, we need to unite for extended periods of prayer, ministry, and service to reach our cities.

It takes 21 days to form a habit. The objective of the "Extreme Days" is to create a heart for God in the life of each participant and mobilize each participant to bring about transformation on their campus. Godly habits are established by living for God one day at a time. One day of sacrifice leads to a 40-day habit of service, which leads to a Lifestyle of selfless love! The following illustration shows us the impact of a sustained campaign:

LORD OF THE FLIES

A pastor in California was walking on the beach one morning. Suddenly, he found himself in the midst of a swarm of flies. Never in all of his walks on the beach had he been under such a barrage of pesky flies. As he thought about the flies, the Holy Spirit asked him,

"What are the names of satan?" He pondered the names from Scripture: liar, father of lies, destroyer, and roaring lion. Then it struck him. Beelzebub is one of the names of Satan, and it means "lord of flies." The Pastor went home and began to study flies. He soon found that the life cycle of a fly is typically 40 days. Therefore, 40 days of sustained treatment is needed to wipe out an infestation of flies.

In citrus areas like Florida, there is a fly called the Mediterranean fruit fly, which can cause major problems and destroy large citrus crops. When an infestation of the Med fly occurs, it is as if everyone is living in a battle-zone. The state declares war on this tiny creature and carries out prolonged aerial and ground assaults. A onetime spraying is useless. To wipe out a complete life cycle of these flies crops must be sprayed for 40-days.

Why so much talk about flies? It is time to go beyond the one-time events. If we want to defeat the "lord of the flies," satan, we must begin prolonged spiritual assaults. The 40 Day campaign is a sustained treatment of Godly influence, powerful prayer, and the love of Christ against satan's destructive strategy on our campuses, neighborhoods, workplaces, and other spheres of influence.

The next critical step in the process of transformation is the fast. For many this is a new and scary thought. We have provided some instruction and encouragement. For many fasting has been a life changing experience.

[WHY SHOULD I FAST?]

Fasting is a sacrifice. You first need to ask God what you should fast. What one thing, if you gave up it for a time, would draw you closer to God?

Fasting Changes Nations.

Throughout history when a nation, a group of people, or an individual sought God with fasting and prayer, God moved in powerful ways and literally changed the course of entire nations. Esther was only a youth when she called the Jews to a fast that changed the world. Daniel had angelic visitation and victory in spiritual realms when he fasted. Israel repeatedly fasted when faced with overwhelming trials. Elijah and Moses both fasted for 40 days. Jesus Himself taught us fasting by His own example.

Fasting is a sacrifice. You first need to ask God what you should fast. Biblical fasts usually included abstaining from all foods though some involved abstaining only from certain types of food. If you are new to fasting, you may ask yourself, "What one thing, if I gave it up for a time, would draw me closer to God?" The first thought of some is, "What is the least I can fast to get by?" Be careful! Desiring to just get by during a fast expresses a shallowness of love for God, a lack of faith in the power of prayer and fasting, and a lack of passionate zeal for change in your home, campus, church, and city. Express your love, faith, and passion for God with a serious sacrifice.

Fasting involves humbling ourselves. James 4:6 "But He gives us more grace." That is why Scripture says: "God opposes the proud but gives grace to the humble." When we humble ourselves under God's hand, God will lift us up.

Fasting leads to gratefulness. We take so much for granted. We expect to have food and be able to eat what we want when we want forgetting that much of the world is hungry every day.

Fasting crucifies our flesh. We begin to acknowledge that we cannot fast in our own strength. We spend so much energy and time eating what we want, when we want it, that when we begin to deny ourselves something, fasting gives us strength to overcome other areas as well.

Fasting at least one area of secular media is very important (TV, radio, internet, newspaper, movies) Be sure to fast something that will help you spend more time with God. The media can consume a lot of our time and energy. Make a commitment to allow God to be the Lord of your use of social media. Allow Him to clean up this area of your life completely if it has been a problem.

The following material on fasting has been adapted from "Fast Forward" by Lou Engle. It has been used by permission.

> *"Fasting begets prophets and strengthens strong men. Fasting makes lawgivers wise; it is the soul's safeguard, the body's trusted comrade, the armor of the champion, the training of the athlete."*
>
> —Basil, Bishop of Caesarea (A.D. 330 - 379).

With the call to enter into extended fasts, we must prepare ourselves adequately so that the fast will honor God and fulfill its purpose. Here are some suggestions to help and encourage you.

1.   When doing any form of substantial fasting of food, seek medical advice and permission before the fast, especially if you have any existing medical concerns or conditions. Remember, **fasting is an attitude of the heart!**

2.   **Fast and pray in order to humble yourself and purify your worship.** In fasting, we are not trying to get something from God, but rather seeking to realign our hearts' affections with His. In fasting we can more readily say, *"We love you, Lord, more than anything in the world."* Any kind of lust is perverted worship, but fasting enables us to cleanse the sanctuary of our hearts from every other rival.

3.   **Don't boast about your fast.** It is fine to let people know you won't be eating, if you need to. What matters is whether the heart is filled with pride or false humility (Matthew 6:16-18).

4.   **Do the fast with someone else.** Two are better than one! We encourage parents and children to consider fasting together. Several generations fasting together has a powerful impact!

5.   **Have a clear target for prayer focus.** Without a vision, (a clear, prayer goal) the people perish. During a fast, have four or five prayer goals that are clearly articulated. When not deeply motivated by a clear goal, you will usually fast until break-fast! Write down your vision, so you can run with it (Habakkuk 2:2).

6.   **Make your commitment and determine the length of your fast.** You can fast in many different ways . . . media fast from TV, movies, and video games. You may want to fast one meal a day, for one whole day, three days or more. Prayerfully consider a 40 day fast of one or more of the following: lunch, web surfing, makeup, red meat, non-Christian music, soft drinks, or sweets. It can be very helpful to choose more than one. We would strongly encourage you to fast everything that pulls you down spiritually. Fast something that will increase your prayer life. Biblical fasts always consisted of food. Therefore, we encourage you to seriously consider the following fasts:

> A Daniel fast of vegetables and/or fruit and water only, is good for those carrying a heavy workload. Fasting "meats and sweets" can be done by athletes who can get protein from other food sources.

> A fruit or vegetable juice fast allows you to enter into fasting but still gives enough energy to function. Many people have done a 40-day juice fast. Out of consideration for your health and metabolism, I would encourage teenagers to use juice and protein drinks for sustenance. If you have sugar sensitivities or problems, consult your physician before attempting this fast.

> A water-only fast has been done by many people. We would not

encourage this kind of fast without strong medical supervision. A water only fast is very difficult, but very powerful and effective. Depending upon your weight and metabolism, you can survive forty days on water alone.

🐷 A total fast is without water. Do Not go beyond three days without water. Discuss your plans with your doctor, and/or church leaders and parents. We do not encourage this type of fast without specific confirmation from the Lord through your church leadership.

7. **Prepare physically.** Two days before you fast, limit your intake of food to fruit and vegetables. Fruit is a natural cleanser and easy to digest. Stop drinking coffee before the fast. Drink lots of water to help your body detoxify. Prepare yourself for mental discomforts such as impatience, crankiness, and anxiety. Expect physical discomforts. You may experience dizziness, headaches, and different kinds of pains. The headaches are not a sign to stop fasting. Your body is working to cleanse itself of impurities.

8. **Take time to pray and read the Word.** This advice may seem obvious, but busyness and distractions can keep you from devotions. Reading books with testimonies of victories gained through fasting will encourage you. Changing History through Prayer and Fasting by Derek Prince, Fast Forward by Lou Engle, and God's Chosen Fast by Author Wallis are recommended.

9. **Expect to hear God's voice in the Word, dreams, visions, and revelations.** Daniel prepared himself to receive revelation through fasting (Daniel 10:1, 2). There is a fasting reward (Matt. 6:18). Some time ago, a Malaysian brother shared how during a forty day fast he was "caught up into the heavens." After the fast, he took a team into the interior of Borneo and saw a dead woman raised to life. Revival broke out in the village as a result of the team's ministry.

10. **Prepare for opposition.** On the day of your fast, you can bet donuts will be in the class or at work. Your spouse will suddenly be inspired to cook your favorite meals. Press through. Many times, you may feel more tension build at home. Satan tempted Jesus during His fast, and we must expect the same. Discouragement may come in like a flood, but recognize the source and take your stand on the victory of Christ.

11. **If you fail, don't give in to condemnation.** The *"to fast or not to fast"* dilemma can be a major tool of the enemy. Even though you may fail several times, God always extends grace. Once, I gave up on a fast. I decided to sneak some yogurt and chips. The next day an intercessor came to me and said, "I saw you in a dream and you were supposed to be fasting, but you were eating yogurt and chips." It was pretty good motivation to start again!

12. **Feel free to rest a lot and continue to exercise with supervision.**

13. **Breakthroughs often come after a fast, not during it.** Do not listen to the lie

that nothing is happening. It is my conviction that every fast done in faith will be rewarded.

14. **Break the fast slowly, over several days with fruit juice or light soups.** On a light juice fast or a water fast your digestive system shuts down. Eating too much too soon can be dangerous. Break the fast with several days of diluted, non-acidic juice, then regular juice, followed by fruit and vegetables. Be careful! May tens of thousands of you fast as God leads you. May you find a greater intimacy with God the Father. May you be used in the greatest revival we have ever seen. Let two generations arise and fulfill this divine mandate! We have taught our children how to feast and play. Now it is time to teach them how to fast and pray!

In the next section, we provide you with helpful training in the four principles applied in the daily assignments. You will need to understand what prayer, servant, and blessing evangelism are. Following that is basic material on "How to Lead a Friend to Christ.

REVOLUTION QUOTES

"Let two generations arise and fulfill this divine mandate! We have taught our children how to feast and play. Now it is time to teach them how to fast and pray!"

—Lou Engle, Author of Fast Forward.

"Fasting begets prophets and strengthens strong men. Fasting makes lawgivers wise; it is the soul's safeguard, the body's trusted comrade, the armor of the champion, the training of the athlete."

—Basil, Bishop of Caesarea (A.D. 330 - 379).

FRIENDSHIP OR BLESSING EVANGELISM

When you bless a person and are used by God to bring that person closer to God, you are practicing **blessing evangelism**. It is relational, rather than instructional. You share yourself, your time and your heart, rather than your knowledge of how to become a Christian. By sharing in this way in the present, you establish the right to share the wonderful message of Jesus in the future.

Key Verse: Proverbs 18:21 "The tongue has the power of life and death."

James 3:9-10 "With the tongue we praise our Lord and Father, and with it we curse men, who have been made in God's likeness. Out of the same mouth come praise and cursing. My brothers, this should not be."

By our words we can turn people away from God, or we can make people thirsty for God. Even Scripture, which should impart life, can be used to wound as well as to heal. Blessing evangelism occurs when we see people as they have been made in the image of God—we see God's potential in a person, and we strive to bring it out.

Jesus spent time with people, and saw in them the image of God. In many biblical accounts Jesus spent time and blessed people who were normally shunned and considered outcasts.

A story is told of a teacher who had extra time one day and gave her class the assignment of writing something positive about each student in the room. She gathered the students' papers, and for each student she compiled a list of encouraging words written about him or her.

Years later when she would meet any of these students, they would show her the wrinkled old note they had clung to all their lives. One of her students was killed in a war, and in his pocket was found the note that he'd carried since that day.

Here are several ways to bless a person:

- Spend time with them, as Jesus did
- Speak encouraging words
- Listen
- Share
- Write a note

[SERVANT EVANGELISM]

Servant evangelism is faith in action. In servant evangelism, we seek to meet the needs of those around us. People are needy. By meeting a person's need, we hope to earn the right to share Jesus with them.

> ***Key Verse: John 20:14-15*** *"Now that I, your Lord and Teacher, have washed your feet, you also should wash one another's feet. I have set you an example that you should do as I have done for you."*

In Jesus' day, washing feet was a practical act of service since people walked barefoot or in sandals wherever they went. Household servants were expected to do this distasteful job. Jesus taught servanthood when He, the King of Kings, washed the feet of His disciples.

How can you be a servant to a people where you live and go to school? It may not go over very well to bring a bucket of water to your classroom, roommate, neighbors, or the workplace and offer to wash people's feet. There is a place for that, but it was a cultural practice that servants did during Jesus' day and your classroom is probably not the place! You could pick up their trash, do their laundry, help with homework, or help with a project. You could help them get to their car when it is raining. Look for practical things that someone has to do. When you see an opportunity to help, ask yourself, *"Why not me? Why not now?"* You also can think of ways to serve your classmates, dorm mates, co-workers, boss, family, friends, and people in church.

When you serve other people, you break through their defenses.

> ***Romans 12:20-21*** *states, "On the contrary: If your enemy is hungry, feed him; if he is thirsty, give him something to drink. In doing this, you will heap burning coals on his head. Do not be overcome by evil, but overcome evil with good."* We can overcome evil done to us by deeds of kindness rather than seeking revenge.

During the next 40 days, you will be asked to serve people in a variety of ways. You don't have to say anything when you serve them. They may ask you why you are serving them – or they may not.

Many times, you may have a chance to explain to them what you are doing. You can tell them something like; *"I just wanted to show you God loves you in a practical way, no strings attached!"*

[PRAYER EVANGELISM]

"Talk to God about your friends before talking to your friends about God." — ED SILVOSO

> **Key Verse: II Corinthians 10:4-5, KJV** *"For the weapons of our warfare are not carnal, but mighty through God to the pulling down of strong holds; casting down imaginations, and every high thing that exalteth itself against the knowledge of God, and bringing into captivity every thought to the obedience of Christ."*
>
> Also, **II Chronicles 7:14** *"If my people, who are called by my name, will humble themselves and pray and seek my face and turn from their wicked ways, then will I hear from heaven and will forgive their sin and will heal their land."* And it is completely in keeping with the spirit of that promise to add, "their campus, home, city or nation"!

Prayer is our most powerful weapon! Prayer is essential in our personal lives as well as in the life of our churches. Without prayer, there is no power. God through our prayers transforms lives. If we want to be a positive influence in our world, we must take prayer seriously. We must humbly approach God and pour out our hearts to Him on behalf of our campus, workplaces, and other spheres of influence. Prayer, like nothing else, has the power to change a person, campus, dorm, workplace, city, state, nation, and the world.

If you are not bold enough to talk to others, but you spend more time in prayer, you may have more influence and power than the one who talks boldly. Keep in mind, with little prayer there is no power.

Pray privately to receive God's power. Pray with a friend. Pray as a group. Pray silently. Pray aloud. Read a prayer from the Bible. Pray from your heart, as you would speak to a friend. Just Pray! Do it often and with a heart for God to change you first, then change others through you.

Believers are praying with wonderful results. They are seeing people healed, marriages restored, lives saved, and their offices turned right side up for God.

Pray! Pray! Pray!

Expect Miracles!

Expect a great God to do great things – through you!

[LEADING A FRIEND TO CHRIST]

Leading a friend to Christ doesn't have to be hard! You may refer to these pages, but we encourage you to memorize the key steps so you can share without the book.

BELIEVE

Key Verse: Acts 16:31 "*They replied, 'believe in the Lord Jesus, and you will be saved—you and your household.'*"

"To believe" in this verse means to put your whole trust in Jesus. The Bible says that we must believe that Jesus Christ died to pay the penalty for our sins, that He rose from the dead, and we must be willing to live for Him.

What we really believe is demonstrated more by what we do than by what we say. Believing in Jesus means turning your life away from sin and going in God's direction rather than your own. It does not mean that we become perfect, but that we are striving to love God and let Him have control of our lives.

REPENT

Key Verse: Luke 13:3 "*. . . But unless you repent, you too will all perish.*"

"To Repent" means: "to turn away from." We have spent most of our lives "doing our own thing" and following our own agendas, often doing things that did not please God. The Bible calls our self-will "sin". "To Repent" means to turn from sin, or to quit following our own agendas, and to choose to follow God's will. We turn away from or give up things that we know displease God, or from anything that He reveals to us. When we turn from sin, we turn to God, and do the things that please Him.

CONFESS YOUR SINS

Key Verse: 1 John 1:9 "*If we confess our sins, he is faithful and just and will forgive us our sins and purify us from all unrighteousness.*"

Confessing sin is more than just saying, "I'm sorry." It is not just being sorry that God doesn't approve of your actions, or being sorry for doing something wrong because you were caught.

Confession means to agree with God's perspective on the matter, agree that what you did was wrong, and that you hate the wrong just as God hates the wrong.

God hates sin, but He still loves the sinner. God delights in forgiving our sins. That's why He sent Jesus to die on the cross for us – to take away our sins. We must recognize our sins and ask for God's forgiveness. What we must to do is ask Jesus into our lives, confess our sins, and receive His forgiveness.

CONFESS JESUS PUBLICLY

Key Verse: Romans 10:9 *"That if you confess with your mouth, 'Jesus is Lord,' and believe in your heart that God raised him from the dead, you will be saved."*

To confess *"Jesus is Lord"* is to make a public declaration that you are a follower of Jesus. Do not be ashamed to tell others that you are a Christian or to follow His example by being baptized.

When you choose to receive Jesus and become a Christian, you need to share this important decision. Tell your friends, your family, and others. Find someone to baptize you. Meet with other believers to pray and encourage one another.

After you share these four main steps and your friend understands them, it may be time to make a decision. Ask him or her, *"Do you want to ask Jesus to come into your life and forgive your sins and save you?"* You may use the sample prayer below to lead him/her through this most important decision.

Dear Jesus, I confess that I have sinned and I believe You died for my sins.

I believe that God raised You from the dead.

I need you to forgive me and cleanse me from my sins.

I am finished with living for me, and I want to live for you.

Please fill me with your Holy Spirit.

Thank you for saving me, for forgiving me, and for cleansing me.

EXTREME DAYS

A STRATEGY FOR AN AWAKENING ON YOUR CAMPUS

ADAPTED FROM:

(ASSIGNMENTS)

Commissioning Day is that special day when you begin the 40-Day Revolution. You declare your intent to be a missionary at your campus, dorm, workplace, apartment, home, and even the world!

It is helpful if you receive a blessing and promise of prayer support from your church family. You will want to choose a "prayer/accountability partner" to pray with you throughout the 40 days. Your prayer partner is an important part of the 40 days, so be sure and choose someone you know will be committed to regularly pray for and with you for the entire 40 days.

COMMISSIONING DAY

Here are some ideas for this very important day.

1. If possible, be commissioned by a pastor or leader. Have them pray over you and ask everyone to pray for you over the next 40 Days.

2. Watch the movie Son of God. (http://www.dutchquest.com/watch-now/) You can watch it alone or invite others to join you. Let this inspire you and build your faith as you begin these next 40 Days. You can watch it free online.

3. Find a prayer/accountability partner

SOCIAL MEDIA ASSIGNMENT - Let the world know about what you're about to start. You could post a link to the website (www.40DayRevolution.com), a picture of the book, and/or share the app. Ask the Lord for a creative way to spread the word and invite others to join you.

A STRATEGY FOR AN AWAKENING ON YOUR CAMPUS

ADAPTED FROM:

REVOLUTION

One woman who was doing the 40-Days at her work prayed for and served her boss during the entire 40-Days. She made him cookies, wrote him notes of encouragement, prayed for him. He had been one of the worst people to work for in the entire organization. By the end of the 40-Days, he was transformed and became a totally transformed person to the point where others commented on his transformation.

Luke 9:1-2 "When Jesus had called the Twelve together, he gave them power and authority to drive out all demons and to cure diseases, and he sent them out to preach the kingdom of God and to heal the sick."

Read: **Acts 1:8, Matthew 22:37-38, Matthew 28:19-20**

JOURNAL

"Ask the Lord what He would have you fast. And, whom he would have you target in prayer and serving during these 40 days?"

_____

_____

_____

REVOLUTIONARY QUOTE

"We need a quickening of faith; faith in the power of the God of Pentecost to convict and convert three thousand in a day. Faith, not in a process of culture by which we hope to train children into a state of salvation, but faith in the mighty God who can quicken a dead soul into life in a moment; faith in moral and spiritual revolution rather than evolution."

—A. C. DIXON

PRAYER

Pray for God to give you courage, strength, and boldness to carry out all of the assignments well

_____

_____

_____

WEEK 1 ~ MEMORY VERSE:

Matthew 22:37-39—The Great Commandment

"Jesus replied: 'Love the Lord your God with all your heart and with all your soul and with all your mind [and with all your strength].' This is the first and greatest commandment. And the second is like it"

David faced Goliath and won a mighty battle. today and over the next 40-Days your going to do the same thing. The difference is your giants are not a man, but the enemy.

GIANT'S DAY

1. Ask God to show you the biggest problems in your life and on your campus (where you live, work, or go to just have fun):

a) Relational conflict	g) Personal sin	m) Alcohol
b) Spiritual apathy	h) Financial trouble	n) Drugs
c) Immorality	i) Addictions	o) Sex
d) Family issues	j) Personal failure	p) Laziness
e) Parenting issues	k) Work-related stress	q) Insecurity
f) Worldliness	l) Partying	r) Others____

2. Pray for these issues. Your prayers can change the spiritual climate of your surroundings.

3. Find a rock and place your rock in a prominent place where you can see it daily window sill, bathroom sink, entrance to room, etc.). It symbolizes the rock with which David killed Goliath, the giant. Let it remind you that your prayers are taking down the giants in your life. Prayer can change the world.

SOCIAL MEDIA ASSIGNMENT - post this verse on Facebook and/or twitter

> *EPHESIANS 6:12 - For we do not wrestle against flesh and blood, but against principalities, against powers, against the rulers of the darkness of this age, against spiritual hosts of wickedness in the heavenly places.*

> *I Samuel 17:45-47 "You come against me with sword and spear and javelin, but I come against you in the name of the Lord Almighty, the God of the armies of Israel, whom you have defied. This day the Lord will hand you over to me, and I'll strike you down and cut off your head. Today ... the whole world will know that there is a God in Israel. All those gathered here will know that it is not by sword or spear that the Lord saves; for the battle is the Lord's, and he will give all of you into our hands."*

EXTREME DAYS
A STRATEGY FOR AN AWAKENING ON YOUR CAMPUS

ADAPTED FROM

40DAY REVOLUTION

JOURNAL

What are the Giants in my life? What do I want God to do in my spheres of influence? What does He want me to do?.

_____

_____

_____

_____

_____

REVOLUTIONARY QUOTE

"Where,oh,where are the eternity-conscious believers? Where are the souls white-hot for God because they fear His holy name and presence and so live with eternity's values in view?" —LEONARD RAVENHILL, REVIVAL GOD'S WAY

PRAYER

Pray about the Giants that you face and that God shows you what are prevalent in your arena.

_____

_____

_____

_____

_____

_____

WEEK 1 ~ MEMORY VERSE:

Matthew 22:37-39—The Great Commandment

"Jesus replied: 'Love the Lord your God with all your heart and with all your soul and with all your mind [and with all your strength].' This is the first and greatest commandment. And the second is like it"

You are called to be a light in the dark. The college life isn't all that Hollywood makes it out to be. It can actually be a very lonely place.

Today, and for the rest of the week pay attention during your classes for the outcasts and the kids no one talks to. Maybe they sit by themselves or are teased. Reach out to them, begin friendships, ask them to sit with you at lunch, and if the opportunity presents itself invite them to church. Find the names of the people you sit next to, and ask how you can be praying for them. Find ways to bless them.

LIGHTHOUSE DAY I - "I PRAY"

SOCIAL MEDIA ASSIGNMENT - Ask this question on either Facebook or twitter saying, "I believe in the power of prayer and want to pray for anyone who has a need today. What can I pray for you about?" You can message individual or post it for everyone to see. Be sure to pray bold prayers that are full of faith regarding the needs people ask you to pray.

> *I Timothy 2:1* *"I urge, then, first of all that requests, prayers, intercession and thanksgiving be made for everyone."*

Prayer Target: Who are the 5 people that you will be focused upon? What are the needs of these 5 or more people?.

Focus 1: _____

Focus 2: _____

Focus 3: _____

Focus 4: _____

Focus 5: _____

EXTREME DAYS
A STRATEGY FOR AN AWAKENING ON YOUR CAMPUS

ADAPTED FROM

40 DAY REVOLUTION

LIGHTHOUSE

1st Period

Your Desk

2nd Period

Your Desk

3rd Period

Your Desk

4th Period

Your Desk

5th Period

Your Desk

6th Period

Your Desk

"God forbid that I should travel with anybody a quarter of an hour without speaking of Christ to them." —GEORGE WHITEFIELD.

PRAYER

Pray for those that God has laid on your heart to focus on during these 40 days..

_____

_____

_____

_____

_____

_____

_____

WEEK 1 ~ MEMORY VERSE:

Matthew 22:37-39—The Great Commandment

"Jesus replied: 'Love the Lord your God with all your heart and with all your soul and with all your mind [and with all your strength].' This is the first and greatest commandment. And the second is like it"

The Bible says, **"pray without ceasing."** Jesus prayed all the time, the Bible says he would pray throughout the night or get up early in the morning to pray.

PRAYER DAY

We have been talking a lot about prayer; it's not just a religious activity. It has power to change the spiritual climate at your school, heal the sick, and raise the dead. Spend as much time today in prayer as possible. When you're not in class or at work be praying, do not watch TV, or hang out with friends unless you are praying together. Set up a time today where everyone doing the 40 Days, or at least your small group, can meet and pray together. Also, talk about how the Revolution is going, share testimonies, and discuss the weekly assignments. You should do this daily or at least weekly.

Stretch yourself. Maybe you've never prayed more than a minute or more than 15 minutes, or no more than an hour. Ask God to help you and lead you and give you the ability to pray more today than you ever have before.

Here is a suggested agenda when you gather to pray with others.

1. Discuss the weekly assignments.

2. Share testimonies.

3. Pray for needs of unbelievers. Pray over the needs of your campus. Pray for unity among the believers. Pray for boldness of believers to share Christ. Pray for the sick.

4. Share your struggles and prayer requests.

5. If your group is large, pray in groups of three. Consider joining arms or hands as you pray.

SOCIAL MEDIA ASSIGNMENT - Invite all of your twitter followers and facebook friends to join in the prayer

JOURNAL

Who came out to pray? Who can I invite to join me in the future?

_____

_____

_____

_____

_____

REVOLUTIONARY QUOTE

"Oh how few find time for prayer! There is time for everything else, time to sleep and time to eat, time to read the newspaper and the novel, time to visit friends, time for everything else under the sun, but no time for prayer, the most important of all things, the one great essential!" —OSWALD SMITH

PRAYER

Of course praying is your main assignment today. Write down the entire subject you are led to pray.

_____

_____

_____

_____

_____

_____

WEEK 1 ~ MEMORY VERSE:

Matthew 22:37-39—The Great Commandment

"Jesus replied: 'Love the Lord your God with all your heart and with all your soul and with all your mind [and with all your strength].' This is the first and greatest commandment. And the second is like it"

Whether it's the administration office or the financial aid there are many staff who work long hours with frustrated and rude students. They also play a very important role in your sphere of influence.

DEAN/ADMINISTRATOR DAY

When you go out of your way to bless, pray, and serve those in authority, it has an amazing impact on their lives. Here are some ways

1. Buy cookies or doughnuts and bring them into one of the offices.
2. Ask how you can pray for them.
3. Write one or more of them an encouraging note.
4. Pray blessings over all of the staff. You can do this from your dorm room, but it is way more powerful if you have the courage to stop by, ask them how you can pray for them, and do it right there and then.
5. If you have been at odds with anyone on staff and in authority try and make amends.

SOCIAL MEDIA ASSIGNMENT - Post something encouraging about your principle

> **Romans 13:1-3** *"Everyone must submit himself to the governing authorities, for there is no authority except that which God has established. The authorities that exist have been established by God. Consequently, he who rebels against the authority is rebelling against what God has instituted, and those who do so will bring judgment on themselves. For rulers hold no terror for those who do right, but for those who do wrong. Do you want to be free from fear of the one in authority? Then do what is right and he will commend you."*

Pray these passages over your leaders.

Ephesians 1:17-20   *Ephesians 3:16-20*
Philippians 1:8-11   *Colossians 1:9-11*
I Thessalonians 3:12-13   *2 Thessalonians 1:1-11*

"When a believing person prays, great things happen."

—JAMES THE LESS / MARTYRED FOR CHRIST / 63A.D.

PRAYER

Spend some time praying for your school president, administrators and others in leadership.

_____

_____

_____

_____

_____

_____

WEEK 1 ~ MEMORY VERSE:

Matthew 22:37-39—The Great Commandment

"Jesus replied: 'Love the Lord your God with all your heart and with all your soul and with all your mind [and with all your strength].' This is the first and greatest commandment. And the second is like it"

Unforgiveness is like pouring a glass of poison to hurt the other person and drinking it yourself. It only hurts you.

FORGIVENESS DAY!
(Seeking forgiveness and giving forgiveness)

First, Jesus encouraged us in the Sermon on the Mount that it is critical to make things right with people whom we have offended. It is more important than even making sacrifices like fasting. Ask God if there is anyone, (students, teachers, parents, coworkers, other family members, etc.) from whom you need to ask forgiveness; then, "Just do it."

• One girl made up with a friend she hadn't spoken to in over a year. They are again best friends.

• One man forgave his father after not speaking to him for 30 years. Then he went to his father's house and told him that he had forgiven him and God worked powerfully in both of their lives.

A great way to begin a conversation with someone whom you need to ask forgiveness of is to say, "I realize I have hurt you or disappointed you with my actions. Will you forgive me?"

Secondly, You may need to forgive someone else. Forgiving can be difficult. No doubt, many of you have been wronged by a parent, child, coworker, friend, relative, or other individual. Some of you have experienced physical, mental, emotional, and/or sexual abuse. God will help you. When you forgive, it helps you heal. Forgiveness is critical.

• One lady forgave a long list of people who had abused her and hurt her and was miraculously healed of 90% deafness and chronic, nearly debilitating back pain.

1. Make a list of people you haven't forgiven. Use a separate piece of paper.

2. Ask God for his help in forgiving them. He will show you.

3. Then with your will, pray, "I will forgive_____."

4. Tear up your list after you have forgiven everyone.

5. Tell each person, if possible, that you have forgiven him/her.

Forgiveness isn't a one-time thing; you may have to continue to forgive these people everyday at first. Eventually Gods healing will take over.

SOCIAL MEDIA ASSIGNMENT - Post this Verse and encourage people to forgive others.

Matthew 5:23-24 "Therefore, if you are offering your gift at the altar and there remember that your brother has something against you, leave your gift there in front of the altar. First go and be reconciled to your brother; then come and offer your gift."

Matthew 6:12 "Forgive us our debts, as we also have forgiven our debtors."

Matthew 6:14-15 "For if you forgive men their trespasses, your heavenly Father will also forgive you. But if you do not forgive men their trespasses, neither will your Father forgive your trespasses."

JOURNAL

From whom do I need to ask for forgiveness? Whom do I need to forgive? Do I need to forgive myself for anything?

_____

_____

_____

_____

_____

_____

REVOLUTIONARY QUOTE

"To be a Christian means to forgive the inexcusable, because God has forgiven the inexcusable in you."

—C.S. Lewis

PRAYER

Take time to forgive those on your list. Also pray for wisdom, boldness, and opportunity to ask forgiveness of any that you need to ask forgiveness of.

_____

_____

_____

_____

_____

_____

WEEK 1 ~ MEMORY VERSE:

Matthew 22:37-39—The Great Commandment

"Jesus replied: 'Love the Lord your God with all your heart and with all your soul and with all your mind [and with all your strength].' This is the first and greatest commandment. And the second is like it"

[ASSIGNMENT]

WEEK 1 ~ DAY 7 ~ SATURDAY ____/____/____
[TODAY'S DATE]

Do you want God to work in power in your life and on your campus? If you said, yes, then take this day very seriously.

DEMOLITION DAY

In the book of Acts, the people of the city of Ephesus burned their occult books that didn't glorify the Lord. I've heard that the equivalent value of what they burned in today's economy would be in the millions of dollars. This led to a great revival and miracles.

Go through your dorm room and get rid of anything that is not glorifying to the Lord. The eyes are the gateway to the soul, honor God by what you watch/listen to/eat. The Bible says that if your right eye causes you to sin you should gouge it out, or basically do what ever it takes to get free from sin.

Look around your dorm room, bedroom, car, living room, work area, play lists (ouch, that hurt), hard drive, etc. and ask Jesus if there is anything which displeases Him that He wants you to get rid of. Then get rid of it! If you find this hard, then ask God to help you love Him more than the things you have that displease Him.

Some students have been led to get rid of

__ CDs	__ Cigarettes	__ Ouija boards/occult
__ Video Games	__ Drugs	__ Videos
__ Magazines	__ Books	__ Cable TV
__ Revealing clothing	__ Social Media	__ Food
__ Sexual Temptations	__ Sports	__ Other_____

Check off things that apply. Don't sell them! Be creative and demolish them.

SOCIAL MEDIA ASSIGNMENT - Post a video on Vine, Instagram, or Facebook of you destroying the things God convicted you about.

> *Acts 19:19* *"Also, many of those who had practiced magic brought their books together and burned them in the sight of all. And they counted up the value of them, and it totaled fifty thousand pieces of silver."*

> *Matthew 5:29* *"If your right eye causes you to stumble, gouge it out and throw it away. It is better for you to lose one part of your body than for your whole body to be thrown into hell."* (Be sure to get your mom's permission before gouging out your eye!)

> *Psalm 119:9-11* *"How can a young man keep his way pure? By living according to your word. I seek you with all my heart; do not let me stray from your commands. I have hidden your word in my heart that I might not sin against you."*

JOURNAL

What needs to be eliminated from my room, home, car or life?

_____

_____

_____

_____

_____

_____

_____

QUOTE

"Some Christians haven't even attempted to think about whether or not they would die for Jesus because they haven't really been living for Him!"

—DC TALK, CHRISTIAN RECORDING ARTIST

PRAYER

Ask God what He would have you get rid of in your room, home, car, playlist, etc. Ask God for the courage and obedience to be able to obey Him completely.

_____

_____

_____

_____

_____

_____

WEEK 1 ~ MEMORY VERSE:

Matthew 22:37-39—The Great Commandment

"Jesus replied: 'Love the Lord your God with all your heart and with all your soul and with all your mind [and with all your strength].' This is the first and greatest commandment. And the second is like it"

As Christians we need to set an example through the way we live and act. We have all heard statistics about pre-marital sex, but the Bible says that looking lustfully is the same as adultery. So, our standard is even greater than that of the worlds.

JOB 31 DAY

The media makes college life look like its all sex, sex, and sex all the time, and that if you don't then there is something wrong with you. Unfortunately, 93% of boys and 62% of girls are exposed to Internet pornography before they enter college. If that wasn't bad enough, 50% of all Christian men and 20% of all Christian women are currently addicted to pornography! If this is something you have struggled with remember God loves you and will forgive your sin. God can set you free.

> **Matthew 5:29** says that "If your right eye causes you to sin you should gouge is out. For it is better for you to lose one part of your body than your whole body to be thrown into hell."

1. If you struggle with pornography get help! Get computer programs like Covenant Eyes, or xxxchurch.com. Delete any apps that you may have used before. If you have to, fast the Internet for a short time.

2. In Job 31:1, Job made a covenant with his eyes not to look at a women lustfully. Do the same, and pray for Gods help and protection over your eyes. Say, "I covenant with my eyes, before God, that I will not let any unwholesome thing into my eyes."

3. If you've had pre-marital sex, ask God's forgiveness, receive His forgiveness, forgive the person you had sex with, break any ungodly soulties. And if you're currently in a physical relationship, seek help from your spiritual leader on how to resolve the problem.

4. Pray against this scheme of the enemy at work in your school.

DECLARE THESE PASSAGES:

> **Job 31:1** - NIV "I made a covenant with my eyes, not to look lustfully at a young woman."

> **Matthew 5:28** "anyone who looks at a women lustfully has already committed adultery with her in his heart."

JOURNAL

What unhealthy soul ties need to be broken in my life? (A soul tie is a relational bond that affects our life; they can be healthy or unhealthy)

_____

_____

_____

_____

_____

_____

_____

_____

REVOLUTIONARY QUOTE

"All God's giants have been weak men, who did great things for God because they believed that God would be with them."

—HUDSON TAYLOR, MISSIONARY TO CHINA

PRAYER

Ask God to break any and all unhealthy soul ties that you have had. Ask God's power to keep your covenant and for freedom if you have been in bondage.

_____

_____

_____

_____

_____

WEEK 2 ~ MEMORY VERSE:

Matthew 28:19-20—The Great Commission

"Therefore go and make disciples of all nations, baptizing them in the name of the Father and of the Son and of the Holy Spirit, and teaching them to obey everything I have commanded you. And surely I [Jesus] am with you always, to the very end of the age."

JERICHO MARCH DAY

Read Joshua 1 and 6. God promised Joshua that if he was bold and courageous to go into the land, God was going to give him every place his foot touched. If you will join with a friend or group of Christians and walk around your dorm, campus, or neighborhood praying for it, you will see God begin to change the spiritual climate.

Prayer walk the entire college campus you attend! Dedicating that land as Gods and asking his presence to come, rule, and reign. If you come across anyone while walking ask if you can pray for them.

1. Pray for the people with whom you live, attend school, and work.

2. Ask God to turn the lost to Christ.

3. Ask God to set free those who are enslaved to addictions.

4. Ask God to put a burning desire -- a fire -- in their hearts for Him.

5. Invite the Holy Spirit to invade the campus.

6. Dedicate the land where you walk to the Lord.

7. Ask people whom God leads you to if you can pray for them and the needs in their life.

DECLARE THESE PASSAGES:

Joshua 6:2-5 *"See, I have delivered Jericho into your hands, along with its king and its fighting men. March around the city once with all the fighting men. Do this for six days. Have seven priests carry trumpets of rams' horns in front of the ark. On the seventh day, march around the city seven times, with the priests blowing the trumpets. When you hear them sound a long blast on the trumpets, have all the people give a loud shout; then the wall of the city will collapse and the people will go up, every man straight in."*

I John 1:7 *"But if we walk in the light, as he is in the light, we have fellowship with one another, and the blood of Jesus, his Son, purifies us from all sin."*

Luke 2:52 *"And Jesus grew in wisdom and stature, and in favor with God and men."*

2 Timothy 1:7, KJV *"For God hath not given us the spirit of fear; but of power, and of love, and of a sound mind."*

SOCIAL MEDIA ASSIGNMENT: Post a picture of you and those who go with you to prayer walk on your campus or neighborhood and challenge others to do the same.

EXTREME DAYS
A STRATEGY FOR AN AWAKENING ON YOUR CAMPUS

ADAPTED FROM

40 DAY REVOLUTION

JOURNAL

Who can you get to prayer walk your campus with you? What did you experience during this time?

_____

_____

_____

_____

_____

REVOLUTIONARY QUOTE

"The church that is arising is stronger, healthier, mightier and capable of transforming our cities by changing the spiritual climate."

—ED SILVOSO, AUTHOR OF THAT NONE SHOULD PERISH & PRAYER EVANGELISM

PRAYER

Pray for boldness in your life. Pray for revival to come to your campus. Pray for all the things listed above in today's assignment.

_____

_____

_____

_____

_____

_____

WEEK 2 ~ MEMORY VERSE:

Matthew 28:19-20—The Great Commission

"Therefore go and make disciples of all nations, baptizing them in the name of the Father and of the Son and of the Holy Spirit, and teaching them to obey everything I have commanded you. And surely I [Jesus] am with you always, to the very end of the age."

As Christians we are called to follow Jesus and to be like Jesus. Nothing epitomizes the life of Jesus more than unconditional love for everyone. By definition, God is love. His love is not conditional upon how you act or what you do. Jesus would talk with total strangers like the woman at the well. He would find ways to relate to them and minister to them and show His Father's love.

WOMAN AT THE WELL DAY

Christians sometimes get a bad rep when it comes to loving sinners or people who believe differently than us. Today show love to everyone you come across, especially the ones it is hard to love. The "weirdoes," the "losers," the "geeks," the "drunks," and the "sluts" all need Gods love, not condemnation. It's time for the labels to go and for us to see people through Jesus' eyes.

1. Pray for opportunities to show love to those who need it. Do as many kind things for people you wouldn't normally relate. A note or words of affirmation go along ways towards cheering someone up and impacting their life..

2. Also, pay attention to anything you say "jokingly" to your friends or anything that could be mean or offensive. Ask the Lord's forgiveness and if necessary anyone whom you have offended.

3. Forgive anyone who bullied you or who did not show love to in the past.

SOCIAL MEDIA ASSIGNMENT - Be an encouragement to people today on social media. Look for opportunities to compliment people and just be a light. Not just close friends and crushes.

> **James 2:1-3** *"My brothers don't show favoritism...If you show special attention to the man wearing fine clothes...have you not discriminated among yourselves and become judges with evil thought?"*

A STRATEGY FOR AN AWAKENING ON YOUR CAMPUS

ADAPTED FROM
40 DAY
REVOLUTION

JOURNAL

Whom can I write a note to today? (A person with whom I wouldn't normally associate and/or a person needing encouragement.)?

_____

_____

_____

_____

_____

REVOLUTIONARY QUOTE

"You cannot do a kindness too soon, for you never know how soon will be too late."
—RALPH WALDO EMERSON

PRAYER

Pray for those whom God leads you to reach out to today.

_____

_____

_____

_____

_____

_____

_____

WEEK 2 ~ MEMORY VERSE:

Matthew 28:19-20—The Great Commission

"Therefore go and make disciples of all nations, baptizing them in the name of the Father and of the Son and of the Holy Spirit, and teaching them to obey everything I have commanded you. And surely I [Jesus] am with you always, to the very end of the age."

Some addictions are less apparent but can be just as debilitating. Some addictions can be to food, video games, work, etc. Ask God if you or someone you love needs freedom in an area of addiction.

JUST SAY NO DAY

The peer pressure begins at an early age to do things that are contrary to God's will. If you're in college, I'm sure you have heard statistics about drug, sex, and alcohol abuse in college. Today we will focus our prayers on freedom in the areas of substance abuse.

- Drugs - 51% have used illegal drugs
- Alcohol - 80% of college students drink
- Drop out - 44% drop out
- Sex - over 70% have had sex and 86% of those have had sex with multiple people.

If you already fit into one or all of these statistics, you may be feeling condemned right now. That is not the goal here. God's love is immeasurable. His mercies are new every morning. That means He forgives us when we ask His forgiveness.

1. Choose not to be a statistic. Choose to honor God by what you do with and put into your body. If you already fit one or more or all then simply ask God's forgiveness, receive it, and commit to allow God to change you, heal you, and empower you.

2. Spend at least 30 minutes praying against substance abuse in your school, home, work place, and the other issues that you see destroying the lives of students.

3. Pray for anyone you know who is struggling in one of these areas. Ask that God open the door for you to help them.

4. If you have struggled in this area, seek help from a spiritual advisor.

5. Make a t-shirt that says you choose not to be a statistic, make it as unique and personal as possible.

SOCIAL MEDIA ASSIGNMENT - Post one or more of these verses and/or a loving prayer for people dealing with addictions.

1 Corinthians 6:19-20 "Do you not know that your bodies are temples of the Holy Spirit, who is in you, whom you have received from God? You are not your own; 20 you were bought at a price. Therefore honor God with your bodies."

Ephesians 5:18 NKJV "And do not be drunk with wine, in which is dissipation; but be filled with the Spirit,"

John 8:36 NKJV "Therefore if the Son makes you free, you shall be free indeed."

JOURNAL

Who do I know that needs prayer to be free of alcohol, drugs, porn, or any other form of addiction?

_____

_____

_____

_____

_____

_____

REVOLUTIONARY QUOTE

"Free will is not the liberty to do whatever one likes, but the power of doing whatever one sees ought to be done, even in the very face of otherwise overwhelming impulse. There lies freedom, indeed." —GEORGE MACDONALD

PRAYER

Focus some of your praying today on those who are struggling with various forms of addiction.

_____

_____

_____

_____

_____

_____

_____

WEEK 2 ~ MEMORY VERSE:

Matthew 28:19-20—The Great Commission

"Therefore go and make disciples of all nations, baptizing them in the name of the Father and of the Son and of the Holy Spirit, and teaching them to obey everything I have commanded you. And surely I [Jesus] am with you always, to the very end of the age."

Everyone knows the professors make or break your class experiences. It's easy to make jokes about professors and to blame them for your bad grades and laziness. In most colleges the class sizes are so big that it can be hard to get to know your professor. Today were going to change that. Today and for the rest of the week you are going to be blessing your professors. Hopefully it will become a lifestyle.

PROFESSOR DAY

You can do one or more of the following:

1. Pray for your Professors. Ask your professor(s) how you can pray for them. Be sure to write down their request and pray for them. Don't be afraid.

2. It is good to give your professor a simple, encouraging note. Some students have included a small gift, a candy bar, or a drink with their note. This can have a powerful impact on their lives. You may want to start with this first to build the openness and relationship even before asking how you can pray for them. Let God lead.

3. Remember to inquire later regarding the prayer request.

4. It is easy to do this for a professor that you like. Try to take extra measures to pray for, bless, and serve those professors that you find harder to like!

6. Instead of complaining about bad professors, start to pray for them. You will be amazed at how they change. Get to know them. Find out their likes, what is bothering them, and pay attention.

7. If you have ever talked bad about a professor repent. If you had a bad relationship with a past professor, ask for their forgiveness.

SOCIAL MEDIA ASSIGNMENT - Go on the website ratemyprofessor.com and write an encouraging and thankful comment and give them a high rating. Professors read those comments, so instead of bashing them encourage them. Also, post something encouraging about your professors anywhere else that you can and tag them.

Galatians 6:6 *"Anyone who receives instruction in the word must share all good things with his instructor."*

JOURNAL

What are my professors needs?

_____

_____

_____

_____

_____

REVOLUTIONARY QUOTE

"This generation of Christians is responsible for this generation of souls on the earth!"

—KEITH GREEN, MUSICIAN & FOUNDER OF LAST DAYS MINISTRIES.

"Work as if everything depended upon your work, and pray as if everything depended upon your prayer."

—WILLIAM BOOTH, FOUNDER OF SALVATION ARMY.

PRAYER

Spend time today praying for each of your professors. Find out specific needs and pray for those.

_____

_____

_____

_____

_____

_____

WEEK 2 ~ MEMORY VERSE:

Matthew 28:19-20—The Great Commission

"Therefore go and make disciples of all nations, baptizing them in the name of the Father and of the Son and of the Holy Spirit, and teaching them to obey everything I have commanded you. And surely I [Jesus] am with you always, to the very end of the age."

During lunchtime it's easy to sit with your friends or the "cool kids," but Jesus shared a meal with Zacchaeus, a tax collector, who was not liked. So today your assignment is to find a Zacchaeus, someone sitting by him or herself and just be friendly. If we are truly going to become like Jesus we need to do what He did.

ZACCHAEUS DAY

Today you are to take an opportunity to share a meal with someone who might not know the Lord.

1. Pray about whom you want to share a meal with today. Maybe it's someone you have already met, or maybe it's a homeless man who lives down the street.

2. Don't feel pressured to start sharing the gospel immediately. If the person asks why you are doing this, just tell them you want to bless them and to show them how much God loves them.

3. One student brought $20 to school and bought lunches for other students. The stories he had and friends he made were amazing.

SOCIAL MEDIA ASSIGNMENT - Add the person that you met on Facebook/Instagram/Twitter/snapchat and post something about how you met this new cool person!

> *Luke 19:5, 9-10 NKJV "And when Jesus came to the place, He looked up and saw him, and said to him, "Zacchaeus, make haste and come down, for today I must stay at your house." ... And Jesus said to him, "Today salvation has come to this house, because he also is a son of Abraham; for the Son of Man has come to seek and to save that which was lost."*

 **EXTREME DAYS**
A STRATEGY FOR AN AWAKENING ON YOUR CAMPUS

ADAPTED FROM
 40 DAY REVOLUTION

JOURNAL

Write about your feelings, experience whether good or bad as you stepped out today and did the assignment.

_____

_____

_____

_____

_____

_____

_____

REVOLUTIONARY QUOTE

"The church gives more time, thought and money to recreation and sports than to prayer."
—SAMUEL CHADWICK

PRAYER

Spend some time praying for the person you met and shared a meal with today.

_____

_____

_____

_____

_____

_____

WEEK 2 ~ MEMORY VERSE:

Matthew 28:19-20—The Great Commission

"Therefore go and make disciples of all nations, baptizing them in the name of the Father and of the Son and of the Holy Spirit, and teaching them to obey everything I have commanded you. And surely I [Jesus] am with you always, to the very end of the age."

[ASSIGNMENT]

You spend a lot of time with roommates, but sometimes you can hardly find time to talk! Sometimes they become your best friend, other times they can make your life miserable. But no one person has a bigger impact on your college experience than your roommate. Today is a day to bless, serve, encourage, and show them how much God loves them.

BLESS YOUR ROOMMATE DAY

1. If you have been at odds with one or more of your roommates about anything make amends. Ask for forgiveness for anything you have done that has bothered or hurt your roommate.

2. Ask them "What can I do to be a better roommate and friend?" Listen to what they say and make changes accordingly.

3. Clean the room for them today. Maybe offer to do their laundry or clean their car. Sometimes it is best to just do something to bless them without asking.

4. If you still live at home, then ask God for ways to bless a family member today.

SOCIAL MEDIA ASSIGNMENT - Post something honoring, encouraging, and thankful about your roommate on social media.

> ***1 Peter 4:10*** *"Each of you should use whatever gift you have received to serve others, as faithful stewards of God's grace in its various forms."*

A STRATEGY FOR AN AWAKENING ON YOUR CAMPUS

ADAPTED FROM

JOURNAL

What are the qualities about your roommate that you appreciate? How can you bless them more?

_____

_____

_____

_____

_____

_____

_____

REVOLUTIONARY QUOTE

"Revival is living the Christ life in the home."

—JAMES A. STEWART

PRAYER

Spend time praying for your roommate.

_____

_____

_____

_____

_____

_____

WEEK 2 ~ MEMORY VERSE:

Matthew 28:19-20—The Great Commission

"Therefore go and make disciples of all nations, baptizing them in the name of the Father and of the Son and of the Holy Spirit, and teaching them to obey everything I have commanded you. And surely I [Jesus] am with you always, to the very end of the age."

In today's fast-paced world we often find little time to talk to the people who live right next door to us. God wants to use you to minister to people in your neighborhood. You are the light. Don't let the light be hidden.

LIGHTHOUSE DAY II - "WE PRAY"

The light dispels the darkness. If you will begin to pray, bless, and serve others around you it will have a powerful impact, begin to dispel the darkness and change the spiritual climate around you.

Today your challenge will be to bless the other students on your floor, your apartment, and in your building by whatever means the Lord leads you to.

1. Prayer walk your building, which means to pray as you walk around the building. Take time to talk to anyone you come across, especially those whom you haven't met yet. Get their name. Ask how they are doing. Ask if there is anything you can pray for them about.

2. Pray that the Lord bless all of the students. Also, pray for opportunities to witness to them.

3. You could write some notes, get a simple gift, like maybe buy doughnuts for your floor, or offer to clean someone's room, just find some way to bless them.

4. Be creative and ask the Lord what He would do to impact those who live around you.

5. Look for a chance to pray with them for a specific need.

   Matthew 22:39 *"Love your neighbor as yourself"*

   Proverbs 18:21 NIV *"The tongue has the power of life and death, and those who love it will eat its fruit."*

SOCIAL MEDIA ASSIGNMENT - Post any testimonies that have happened so far, or what God has been teaching you the past two weeks.

A STRATEGY FOR AN AWAKENING ON YOUR CAMPUS

ADAPTED FROM 40 DAY REVOLUTION

JOURNAL

Lord, how do you want me to minister to people around me today? Who do you want me to minister to?

_____

_____

_____

_____

_____

_____

_____

_____

REVOLUTIONARY QUOTE

"The only way to persevere in prayer is to burn every other bridge."

COREY RUSSELL, PRAYER: WHY OUR WORDS TO GOD MATTER

PRAYER

Pray for opportunities, divine appointments to arise as you prayer walk. Pray for the people God shows you and leads you to

_____

_____

_____

_____

_____

_____

WEEK 3 ~ MEMORY VERSE:

Proverbs 18:21, KJV—Blessing Evangelism

"Death and Life are in the power of the tongue; and they that love it shall eat the fruit thereof."

Whenever an army strategically plans to take over a city, it locates the gates or the entry points into the city. **Controlling** what goes in and out provides a powerful advantage.

STORM THE GATES DAY

It is time for us to seize that powerful advantage over our campuses, neighborhoods and cities, by praying in front of the gates or entry points into the schools, homes, and neighborhoods.

1. Pray in front of your school's main doorway and before the doors of your home.

2. Ask God to come and rule, to bring His protection, and to set angels as guards on your campus and home.

3. Some have chosen to anoint the door with oil to symbolize a dedication of the campus to God.

4. Ask for God's mercy on those who have sinned. Pray that any curses on your campus and home would be broken.

5. Ask God to guard the school and your home from evil and to prevent lies from being able to take root in people's lives.

SOCIAL MEDIA ASSIGNMENT -Your social media accounts are the gates to your beliefs. Take today to clean up all your accounts to glorify the lord. Delete pictures that don't glorify God. Delete likes or posts that God leads you to.

Genesis 24:60 ". . . may your offspring possess the gates of their enemies."

Isaiah 26:2 "Open the gates that the righteous nation may enter, the nation that keeps faith."

Matthew 16:16-18 ". . . You are the Christ, the Son of the living God." ". . . And on this rock I will build my church and the gates of Hades will not overcome it."

EXTREME DAYS
A STRATEGY FOR AN AWAKENING ON YOUR CAMPUS

ADAPTED FROM

40 DAY REVOLUTION

JOURNAL

Where are the gateways to my campus, workplace, and home? Lord, how do you want me to pray regarding these gateways?

_____

_____

_____

_____

_____

QUOTE

"When a nation calls its prime men to battle, homes are broken, weeping sweethearts say their goodbyes, businesses are closed, college careers are wrecked, factories are refitted for wartime production. Rationing and discomforts are accepted—all for war.

Can we do less for the greatest fight that this world has ever known outside of the cross—this end-time siege on sanity, morality and spirituality?"

—LEONARD RAVENHILL

PRAYER

Today you will pray over all the entry points in your life. Write out a prayer to claim those gateways.

_____

_____

_____

_____

IMPORTANT NOTE: Tomorrow is cookie and doughnuts day. Plan ahead!

WEEK 3 ~ MEMORY VERSE:

Proverbs 18:21, KJV—Blessing Evangelism

"Death and Life are in the power of the tongue; and they that love it shall eat the fruit thereof."

Today's assignment will cost you some money and time, but it will be a blast. **Serving OTHERS** always costs us. Today your going to bake or buy cookies, doughnuts, or what ever treat you feel like, and then just give them away no strings attached! This assignment is really fun when done as a group.

COOKIES/DOUGHNUTS DAY

1. Bake or buy cookies, doughnuts, or other baked goods and give them away.
2. You can give them away to people in your dorm or get to class early and distribute the goodies.
3. Tell people, "This is just to show you God loves you in tangible ways."
4. Ask them if they need prayer for anything.

SOCIAL MEDIA ASSIGNMENT - Post this verse.

> *Matthew 5:16 ESV* *"In the same way, let your light shine before others, so that they may see your good works and give glory to your Father who is in heaven."*

> *John 13:15* *"I have set for you an example that you should do as I have done for you."*

EXTREME DAYS
A STRATEGY FOR AN AWAKENING ON YOUR CAMPUS

ADAPTED FROM

 40 DAY REVOLUTION

JOURNAL

How did you impact others today when you gave them something to eat?

_____

_____

_____

_____

_____

_____

REVOLUTIONARY QUOTE

"Blessings are more powerful than curses because curses can be broken. In the celestial poker game, a hand of blessings always beats a hand of curses."

—ED SILVOSO, FOUNDER AND DIRECTOR OF HARVEST EVANGELISM

PRAYER

Today we encourage you to pray for everyone you met while giving away something to eat.

_____

_____

_____

_____

_____

_____

WEEK 3 ~ MEMORY VERSE:

Proverbs 18:21, KJV—Blessing Evangelism

"Death and Life are in the power of the tongue; and they that love it shall eat the fruit thereof."

During the 40 days you are challenged to be missionaries on your college campus. Well today your going after another missions field, your work place. Maybe you're not working today, and that's ok, but the next shift you have I want you to look at it in a different way..

WORK PLACE DAY

Look at is as an opportunity to share the love of God with your coworkers, your boss, and the customers who enter your store.

1. Pray for opportunities to witness to costumers and coworkers today.

2. Begin praying for your work place. That the spiritual climate would change and that you would begin to see God working there.

3. If you have had animosity with anyone at work, or any kind of strife, begin to repair that relationship. First forgive them, and then show them love.

4. Be a light by your work habits. Be the hardest worker, and do things without being told. Set an example so that your life shows God.

5. If you don't have a job then ask the Lord to show you somewhere equivalent in your life where you can begin to change the spiritual atmosphere by prayer, serving others and blessing others.

SOCIAL MEDIA ASSIGNMENT - Post this verse

> *John 13:35* *"By this everyone will know that you are my disciples, if you love one another," and/or post something encouraging about the people you work with.*

EXTREME DAYS
A STRATEGY FOR AN AWAKENING ON YOUR CAMPUS

ADAPTED FROM
40 DAY REVOLUTION

JOURNAL

What does God want to do to bring transformation to my workplace through me?

_____
_____
_____
_____
_____
_____

REVOLUTIONARY QUOTE

""A new breed of marketplace missionaries is emerging: men and women who dare believe that the same salvation that transforms the soul can also change society, beginning with their sphere of influence.""

—ED SILVOSO

PRAYER

Pray for all the employees with whom you work. Find out their needs, pray and follow up.

_____
_____
_____
_____
_____
_____

WEEK 3 ~ MEMORY VERSE:

Proverbs 18:21, KJV—Blessing Evangelism

"Death and Life are in the power of the tongue; and they that love it shall eat the fruit thereof."

College is unfortunately a time when many people fall away from serving the Lord. It's easy to be led astray by the parties and cute boys and girls, by persuasive professors, and a myriad of other things. So today is a day you call straying believers back to God.

M.I.A. (MISSING IN ACTION) DAY

Start by praying for anyone you know who has fallen away from God. Invite them back to your Christian club, a Bible study, or your church. Do it in a loving way. Remember that anything God leads you to do must be done with humility, love, and a desire to restore individuals to faith. Many people have been spiritually wounded. Do not condemn or be judgmental.

Here are some things you could do.

1. Pray for people you know who are M.I.A.

2. Speak an encouraging word to them.

3. Listen to his or her story about how they were wounded. Pray for God to heal their heart

4. Write a note to encourage them.

5. Try to build a relationship with them, so you can have a platform to invite them back.

SOCIAL MEDIA ASSIGNMENT -Invite your twitter Followers and Facebook Friends to join you at church this coming week! Offer to give any of them a ride if they can't drive. If they can't come, you can at least give them the link to the service.

> **Galatians 6:1-2** *"Brothers, if someone is caught in a sin, you who are spiritual should restore him gently. But watch yourself, or you also may be tempted. Carry each other's burdens, and in this way you will fulfill the law of Christ."*

A STRATEGY FOR AN AWAKENING ON YOUR CAMPUS

ADAPTED FROM

JOURNAL

Ask God who are the M.I.A.s and how can you bless them?

_____

_____

_____

_____

_____

_____

REVOLUTIONARY QUOTE

"The whole history of the Church is one long story of this tendency to settle down on this earth and to become conformed to this world, to find acceptance and popularity here and to eliminate the element of conflict and of pilgrimage. That is the trend and the tendency of everything. Therefore outwardly, as well as inwardly, pioneering is a costly thing."

—T. AUSTIN SPARK

PRAYER

Pray for the people whom God leads you to who have been M.I.A. Pray for them to be restored to faith, a relationship with God and fellowship with other believers.

_____

_____

_____

_____

_____

WEEK 3 ~ MEMORY VERSE:

Proverbs 18:21, KJV—Blessing Evangelism

"Death and Life are in the power of the tongue; and they that love it shall eat the fruit thereof."

Food is a blessing that many Americans take for granted, when in reality most of the world and a large percentage of Americans aren't sure where there next meal is coming from.

I WAS HUNGRY DAY

You are halfway there! Renew your commitment to the 40 days and focus! For the next 7 weekdays you will be ministering to Jesus in practical ways. Read Matthew 25:31-46.

It's amazing how many college students don't have enough money to eat. So today were going to serve Jesus by serving others. Pay for someone's meal, take someone out for lunch, or buy someone groceries. If you don't know of anyone who is in need just go down the street to the homeless man. Buy him a meal and then sit there with him while he eats and just show Gods love.

1. You could fast lunch and use the money you save to buy someone else a lunch.

   a. If the person asks why, say "Just because I want you to know that God loves you in a practical way, no strings attached."

   b. If the person wants you to sit with him/her, then do so and pray for a chance to share more about God's love with him/her.

2. Buy a meal for a homeless person. Take them to a restaurant or buy the food and take it to them.

3. Make a meal for a needy student, individual, or family or buy them some groceries.

4. Send some money to a famine relief program.

SOCIAL MEDIA ASSIGNMENT - Post this verse:

> **Matthew 25:35,40** *"For I was hungry and you gave me something to eat . . . whatever you did for one of the least of these brothers of mine, you did for me."*

EXTREME DAYS

A STRATEGY FOR AN AWAKENING ON YOUR CAMPUS

ADAPTED FROM

JOURNAL

Ask the Lord, what can I do to feed the hungry today or on a regular basis?

_____

_____

_____

_____

_____

_____

REVOLUTIONARY QUOTE

"By the time the average Christian gets his temperature up to normal, everybody thinks he has a FEVER!"

—WATCHMAN NEE, CHINESE AUTHOR AND LEADER

PRAYER

Pray for people who are hungry, those all over the world who will not be able to eat today. Pray for the homeless and the families around you who don't have enough food.

_____

_____

_____

_____

_____

_____

WEEK 3 ~ MEMORY VERSE:

Proverbs 18:21, KJV—Blessing Evangelism

"Death and Life are in the power of the tongue; and they that love it shall eat the fruit thereof."

Your **RA**, or whatever term you use for the person overseeing your dorm, may be the coolest person ever, until clean room checks come. That's when it gets tough. Maybe you live in an apartment. Often there are people who manage your apartment building. These people are Often work hard for little compensation, so today do something to honor and bless them, speak words of encouragement. Ask how you can help and what you can do for him or her.

BLESS YOUR RA/LANDLORD DAY

Maybe you don't live on campus; well you can still bless your landlord. Even if you still live at home you can bless and serve your parents, they most likely let you live at home for free or at least a great deal. Today, go out of your way to clean the house and bless them today.

1. Pray blessing for your RA or landlord. Ask them how you can pray for them, pray, and then follow up.

2. Write an encouraging note for them. A few words of appreciation and kindness go a long way.

3. Serve them in some way. Clean your place as if Jesus were the honored guest tonight.

SOCIAL MEDIA ASSIGNMENT - Post something encouraging about you RA or Landlord on Facebook or twitter.

A STRATEGY FOR AN AWAKENING ON YOUR CAMPUS

ADAPTED FROM
40 DAY REVOLUTION

JOURNAL

What would the Lord have you do today to bless those who have oversight of your residence?

_____

_____

_____

_____

_____

_____

REVOLUTIONARY QUOTE

"When the high point of Christian celebration is the fact that we have done something that is humanly possible, something that we can do without God, no matter how noble it is, then we are at a real low point in Christian manifestation and demonstration. Our assignment is to invade the impossible – those things that cannot be accomplished without God."

— BILL JOHNSON, MANIFESTO FOR A NORMAL CHRISTIAN LIFE

PRAYER

Pray blessings, encouragement over those who have care over our residence, like your RA or landlord.

_____

_____

_____

_____

_____

_____

WEEK 3 ~ MEMORY VERSE:

Proverbs 18:21, KJV—Blessing Evangelism

"Death and Life are in the power of the tongue; and they that love it shall eat the fruit thereof."

[ASSIGNMENT]

LIGHTHOUSE DAY III - "SERVE SOMEBODY DAY"

Jesus lived a life of servitude. Mark 10:45 (NIV) says, "For even the Son of Man did not come to be served, but to serve, and to give his life as a ransom for many." So today is about serving everyone in humility, not expecting anything in return. Everywhere you go, and everyone you come in contact with look for opportunities to serve them!

Here are some things you could do: Help out a professor, carry someone's trays for them in the cafeteria, clean someone's room, pay for someone's food, or what ever the Lord leads you to do. If you spend your day looking for ways to bless, serve, and help everyone you come in contact with you will end up being the one blessed today. Let this not end today, but let serving become a lifestyle you live.

> **James 1:27** *"Religion that God our Father accepts as pure and faultless is this; to look after orphans and widows in their distress and to keep oneself from being polluted by the world."*

SOCIAL MEDIA ASSIGNMENT - Pray as you go onto your social media today for the Lord to show you those who look like they need someone to love them and serve them, and then seek to minister to them or meet their need.

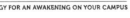

A STRATEGY FOR AN AWAKENING ON YOUR CAMPUS

ADAPTED FROM

JOURNAL

Whom you could serve today in a special way and what would the Lord have you do?

_____

_____

_____

_____

_____

_____

REVOLUTIONARY QUOTE

"Now that I your Lord and Teacher, have washed your feet, you also should wash one another's feet. I have set you an example that you should do as I have done for you."

—JESUS (John 20:14-15)

PRAYER

Pray for divine appointments of opportunities to serve others. Ask God to open your eyes to their needs and how you could minister to them.

_____

_____

_____

_____

_____

_____

IMPORTANT NOTE: Tomorrow is "I Was Thirsty Day." Plan ahead!

WEEK 4 ~ MEMORY VERSE:

John 13:14-15—Servant Evangelism

"Now that I, your Lord and Teacher, have washed your feet, you also should wash one another's feet. I have set you an example that you should do as I have done for you."

People feel more comfortable receiving drinks if the beverages are in closed containers.

I WAS THIRSTY DAY

As mentioned on Day 20, this week you will be serving Jesus by serving others. It may cost you a little bit, but this week will be a blast, and it will bear a lot of fruit. Today you will give a drink to those who are thirsty. Remember that the greatest thirst people have is for living water. By serving them you will make them even thirstier for the truth.

Today you will give a drink to those who are thirsty. Remember that the greatest thirst people have is for living water. By serving them you will make them even thirstier for the truth.

See if you can coordinate with a ministry leader and other students from any Christian group that you are part of. Make a sacrifice, don't do "just enough." Challenge your self and make a sacrifice; people will respond.

The following are some ideas that you could use:

1. Buy drinks for others and give them away at school, in your dorm, in your neighborhood, or at a sporting event.

2. It would be great to fill up a cooler with drinks, lemonade, and water. Bring cups for the drinks.

3. Tell people that what Jesus has can really satisfy the thirst in their souls and spirit. Alternatively, tell them that you used to be thirsty, but not anymore, because Jesus satisfied your spiritual thirst.

4. Give a drink to your teacher, your mom, your dad, your boss, your friend, a stranger, and anyone God shows you who are thirsty. Some have put a drink in their mailbox with a note to the mail delivery person. Be creative.

5. Identify your local church, campus club, or Bible Study group on a little address card as you hand out the drink.

SOCIAL MEDIA ASSIGNMENT - Post this scripture.

> ***Matthew 25:35b & 40*** *". . . I was thirsty and you gave me something to drink . . . The king will reply, 'I tell you the truth, whatever you did for one of the least of these brothers of mine, you did for me.'*

A STRATEGY FOR AN AWAKENING ON YOUR CAMPUS

ADAPTED FROM
40 DAY REVOLUTION

Will I do this assignment alone or with a group? Whom can I serve by giving them a drink today?

_____

_____

_____

_____

_____

_____

REVOLUTIONARY QUOTE

"We have given too much attention to methods and to machinery and to resources, and too little to the Source of Power, the filling of the Holy Ghost."

—J. HUDSON TAYLOR, FOUNDER OF CHINA INLAND MISSION

PRAYER

Pray for divine appointments as you seek to give out drinks and then pray for those whom you have opportunities to meet and serve today.

_____

_____

_____

_____

_____

_____

WEEK 4 ~ MEMORY VERSE:

John 13:14-15—Servant Evangelism

"Now that I, your Lord and Teacher, have washed your feet, you also should wash one another's feet. I have set you an example that you should do as I have done for you."

[ASSIGNMENT]

On a college campus there are many strangers, a lot of people who look different and act different then you. So today you will serve Jesus by reaching out to a stranger.

I WAS A STRANGER DAY

There are many ways that you could do this. Pay attention to how many people walk alone, eat alone, and barely leave their dorm rooms. Instead of ignoring them show them love, even just having a conversation or saying something nice can impact them. Ask God to give you a creative way to invite a stranger into your life, circle of friends, or church. Something nice can impact them.

1. Ask God to show you a stranger who needs someone to reach out to him or her and to reveal how you can bless him or her.

2. Invite your new friend to your table for lunch.

3. Invite them into your dorm or your circle of friends.

4. Meet a new dorm mate or neighbor, or someone who you may have lived next to for years but never met.

5. If you don't feel the Holy Spirit leading you towards someone, there is always that kid who sits by himself during lunch. Go talk to him and sit with him, or invite him to sit with you.

SOCIAL MEDIA ASSIGNMENT - Post this scripture.

> **Matthew 25:35a & 40** "... I was a stranger and you invited me in ... The King will reply, 'I tell you the truth, whatever you did for one of the least of these brothers of mine, you did for me.'

EXTREME DAYS

A STRATEGY FOR AN AWAKENING ON YOUR CAMPUS

ADAPTED FROM
40DAY
REVOLUTION

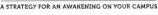

JOURNAL

What ways could I bless, serve, pray for, or tell a stranger of God's love today? Who is a stranger to me in my neighborhood or at work?

_____

_____

_____

_____

_____

_____

REVOLUTIONARY QUOTE

"We socialists would have nothing to do if you Christians had continued the revolution begun by Jesus."

—SPOKEN IN THE 1920S BY A LEADING SOCIALIST

PRAYER

Pray for the person whom God led you to today. Write down their needs, pray over those needs, and then follow up with them.

_____

_____

_____

_____

_____

_____

WEEK 4 ~ MEMORY VERSE:

John 13:14-15—Servant Evangelism

"Now that I, your Lord and Teacher, have washed your feet, you also should wash one another's feet. I have set you an example that you should do as I have done for you."

Believe that God not only *can* heal the sick, but that He *will* heal the sick.

I WAS SICK AND YOU VISITED DAY

Today we're going to challenge you to get outside your comfort zone. Jesus sent out the multitudes to Heal the sick, I believe He meant that literally! So today anyone you come across who is sick, injured, limping, or has any pain in his or her body pray for them. If this is something your not use to doing that's ok, you will get more comfortable with it the more that you do it!

1. Pray for the sick you encounter today while at class, work, or while your eating.
2. Tell them you believe in the power of prayer and that you want to show them how much God loves them.
3. HAVE FAITH!!!! Believe that God can and will heal the sick.
4. Visit anyone you know who is in the hospital or sick. Take care of them and be a servant to them.
5. Read Mark 16:14-20 James 5:13-20 Matthew 10:5-10 Acts 6:8
6. If you would like some more training on how to heal the sick watch someone like Bill Johnson or Todd White on YouTube.

SOCIAL MEDIA ASSIGNMENT - Ask if there is anyone who you can pray for on social media, and ask people to post testimonies of healings!

> *Matthew 25:36b, 40* *"I was sick and you looked after me." ". . . I tell you the truth, whatever you did for one of the least of these brothers of mine, you did for me."*

A STRATEGY FOR AN AWAKENING ON YOUR CAMPUS

ADAPTED FROM

 REVOLUTION

JOURNAL

Ask the Lord how He would want you to minister to someone who is sick today and who that might be. Write down their needs and what you experienced ministering to them today.

_____

_____

_____

_____

_____

_____

REVOLUTIONARY QUOTE

". . . in this night the dawn is about to break . . . God is recruiting an army of recklessly abandoned youth, completely devoted to Himself. They know what it is to love much because they have been forgiven much."

—LOU ENGLE, YOUTH EVANGELIST AND AUTHOR

PRAYER

You will be praying for those who are sick today, be sure to write down their needs and follow up to show them you care.

_____

_____

_____

_____

_____

_____

WEEK 4 ~ MEMORY VERSE:

John 13:14-15—Servant Evangelism

"Now that I, your Lord and Teacher, have washed your feet, you also should wash one another's feet. I have set you an example that you should do as I have done for you."

Its amazing how much excess we have here in America, count how many pairs of shoes you have. How many do you have? 5? 10? 20? Did you know that 40% of the world does not own a single pair of shoes?

YOU CLOTHED ME DAY

Today your assignment is to go through all of your clothes and get rid of the excess, give it away to homeless ministries and the needy.

1. Clean out your closet and give clothes away to the needy.

2. Buy something nice for someone who may not have much. Maybe you even know a student who doesn't have much, leave the gift of some of your clothes with an anonymous note.

3. If you don't believe you have any excess and you barely have enough clothes for yourself that's okay. Start a clothing collection for a local charity at school, in your church, or in your neighborhood.

4. Find a homeless person. Find out that person's shoe size, shirt or pant size, and buy them something. Remember, some have given to angels without knowing it. Serve others as if they were Jesus.

Go to http://p1124.storenvy.com/, they sell clothes that are meant to be given away. Once you have given them away they send you another of the same thing free of charge.

SOCIAL MEDIA ASSIGNMENT - You could post the verse above or encourage your friends to go through their closets and bring the clothes to you so you can take them to a clothing ministry.

> **Matthew 25:36a, 40** "I needed clothes and you clothed me.". . . I tell you the truth, whatever you did for one of the least of these brothers of mine, you did for me."

A STRATEGY FOR AN AWAKENING ON YOUR CAMPUS

ADAPTED FROM
40 DAY
REVOLUTION

JOURNAL

Ask Jesus what He would have you give and where you should give it.?

_____

_____

_____

_____

_____

_____

QUOTE

"We Christians have given Calvary to the Communists. They accept deprivation and death to spread their gospel, while we Christians reject any gospel that does not major on healing and happiness."

—GEORGE E. FAILLING

PRAYER

Pray for the person or people whom God leads you to give to today.

_____

_____

_____

_____

_____

_____

WEEK 4 ~ MEMORY VERSE:

John 13:14-15—Servant Evangelism

"Now that I, your Lord and Teacher, have washed your feet, you also should wash one another's feet. I have set you an example that you should do as I have done for you."

College is a time when a lot of people find themselves in trouble with the law. Underage drinking, drugs, and even rape are just some of the things that plague college campuses.

I WAS IN PRISON AND YOU VISITED ME DAY

Well today your job is to show them all love. If you know of someone who was arrested, try and visit him or her, or at least write him or her a letter. Even if you two weren't close or you didn't even know them that letter could mean the world to them. If you don't know of anyone that's okay, spend the day praying for the persecuted church around the world. Visit a website that talks about the persecuted church. Pray for your brothers and sisters in Christ who are being beaten, thrown in prison and killed for the faith.

1. If you can, visit someone you know who is currently in jail or prison.

2. Send them a Christian book or magazine, and write them an encouraging note.

3. Pray for the persecuted church around the world. 322 Christians die every month, pray for their safety and protection.

4. Pray for those who are prisoners outside of prison. People who are tormented and feel that there is no escape. Pray that your eyes would be open to these people so that you can help them and tell them of the joys of Jesus Christ.

SOCIAL MEDIA ASSIGNMENT - Post this scripture.

> **Matthew 25:36c, 40** *"I was in prison and you came to visit me . . . I tell you the truth, whatever you did for one of the least of these brothers of mine, you did for me."*

JOURNAL

Take a few minutes to put yourself in the shoes of someone who is in prison. Imagine what they go through. Write down your thoughts. This will help you pray.

_____

_____

_____

_____

_____

_____

REVOLUTIONARY QUOTE

"Remember the Lord's people who are in jail and be concerned for them. Don't forget those who are suffering, but imagine that you are there with them."

—PAUL THE APOSTLE (HEBREWS 13:2, CEV)

PRAYER

Spend time today praying for those who are in prison and for the persecuted believers around the world.

_____

_____

_____

_____

_____

_____

WEEK 4 ~ MEMORY VERSE:

John 13:14-15—Servant Evangelism

"Now that I, your Lord and Teacher, have washed your feet, you also should wash one another's feet. I have set you an example that you should do as I have done for you."

[ASSIGNMENT] WEEK 4 ~ DAY 28 ~ SATURDAY ____/____/____
[TODAY'S DATE]

If you have failed to be involved with other believers and or attend church, ask God's forgiveness and find out about a church, Bible study, or Christian club that you could get involved in.

LIGHTHOUSE DAY IV - TAKE A FRIEND TO CHURCH DAY

In some ways, the last 28 days have been leading up to this. Invite everyone you have been blessing, praying for, and reaching out to for the last 4 weeks to your church, or bible study, or Christian club. Offer to drive them so they don't have any excuses. It may not work for them to join you at church tomorrow so plan on the next week if you have to. If possible let your pastor know that guests will be attending.

SOCIAL MEDIA ASSIGNMENT - Post something on your mom's wall about how much you love her and what she means to you.

> **Hebrews 10:25** *"And let us not neglect our meeting together, as some people do, but encourage one another, especially now that the day of his return is drawing near."*

EXTREME DAYS
A STRATEGY FOR AN AWAKENING ON YOUR CAMPUS
ADAPTED FROM 40 DAY REVOLUTION

JOURNAL

Whom can I begin to invite to come with me to church?

_____

_____

_____

_____

_____

_____

REVOLUTIONARY QUOTE

""I go to church as an expression of my need for God and for God's family."
—PHILIP YANSEY

PRAYER

Pray for your church and pray for people whom you know need to be involved with other believers. Pray for divine appointments and boldness to invite others to church.

_____

_____

_____

_____

_____

_____

IMPORTANT NOTE: Tomorrow is "Take A Friend to Curch Day." Plan ahead!

WEEK 4 ~ MEMORY VERSE:

John 13:14-15—Servant Evangelism

"Now that I, your Lord and Teacher, have washed your feet, you also should wash one another's feet. I have set you an example that you should do as I have done for you."

God gives us some great promises when we will honor our father and mother. So even if you have a strained relationship with your parents do something today to honor them.

 FAMILY DAY

If you live on campus odds are you don't see your family a whole lot. Shoot, even if you still live at home, you're probably so busy with school, work, friends, and sleep that you don't spend a whole lot of quality time with them. Well, today you're going to change that. You have spent the last 4 weeks blessing others; today is all about your family.

1. If you still live at home do chores, clean around the house. Spend today hanging out and doing what your family members like to do.

2. If you don't live at home call your mom, dad, brothers, and sisters just to talk and hear how they are doing. Talk about what God is doing in your life, and how much you miss them.

3. Write everyone in your family an encouraging note about how much you love them and all of their best qualities. If you don't live with them send it to them in the mail.

4. Think of anything else you can do to bless and honor your family.

5. If you have been at odds with anyone in your family make amends. Ask for forgiveness for anything you have done to hurt anyone in your family. If they have hurt you, forgive them. Ask God to help you if that is challenging.

SOCIAL MEDIA ASSIGNMENT - Post something encouraging about your family for the world to see.

> *Ephesians 6:2-3* *"HONOR YOUR FATHER AND MOTHER (which is the first commandment with a promise). So that it may be well with you, and that you may live long on the earth."*

JOURNAL

What are the things that I appreciate about my parents? How can I show them honor and love today?

_____

_____

_____

_____

_____

_____

REVOLUTIONARY QUOTE

"A man ought to live so that everybody knows he is a Christian…and most of all his family ought to know."

~ D.L. MOODY

PRAYER

Pray for your parents today. Find out what their needs are and spend time praying over those needs. If you can, pray with them, even if it has to be over the phone or Skype.

_____

_____

_____

_____

_____

WEEK 5 ~ MEMORY VERSE:

II Corinthians 10:4,5, KJV—Prayer Evangelism

"For the weapons of our warfare are not carnal, but mighty through God to the pulling down of strong holds; casting down imaginations, and every high thing that exalteth itself against the knowledge of God, and bringing into captivity every thought to the obedience of Christ."

In this modern day and age, we have a million of distractions right at our fingertips. Sometimes it's hard to CHOOSE God over entertainment, or CHOOSE God over friends.

BE WITH ME DAY

Today your going to CHOOSE God over everything, any moment you are not in class or at work you will spend with Christ, no TV, no friends, no sports, no phone just God. That means when you wake up you read your bible, when you are in the car you're listening to your bible or praying. You should be able to CHOOSE God for at least one day. Make sure you spend equal amount of time praying and listening to his voice and not just reading your bible!!!!

1. Get up 30 minutes earlier so you can read your bible and start your day off right.

2. While walking or driving to school put an audio bible on. Many apps have this feature!

3. Bring your Bible to school and during your lunch break read it! It could be a great conversation starter.

4. After school and homework don't go straight to your computer or TV. Put away the electronics and spend some quality time with God. Take time to read your Bible, listen to what God has to say and right down what ever he speaks to you.

5. Pay attention to the things you would normally have done with your time, are they glorifying towards God?

SOCIAL MEDIA ASSIGNMENT - Fast (Don't go on) social media all day, instead spend the time with God. You will survive.

EXTREME DAYS
A STRATEGY FOR AN AWAKENING ON YOUR CAMPUS

ADAPTED FROM
40 DAY REVOLUTION

JOURNAL

What struggles do I face in trying to spend an entire day with God? What can I do about those hindrances?

_____

_____

_____

_____

_____

_____

REVOLUTIONARY QUOTE

"Every promise, every command in the Bible will be misunderstood unless we interpret it in the light of the Lord's command to Win the World for Him."

—ED SILVOSO

PRAYER

Spend time writing out your prayers to God. Ask Him about things in your life. Write what He speaks to you.

_____

_____

_____

_____

_____

_____

WEEK 5 ~ MEMORY VERSE:

II Corinthians 10:4,5, KJV—Prayer Evangelism

"For the weapons of our warfare are not carnal, but mighty through God to the pulling down of strong holds; casting down imaginations, and every high thing that exalteth itself against the knowledge of God, and bringing into captivity every thought to the obedience of Christ."

"Don't complain to yourselves that you can't go to the mission field! Thank God for bringing the **mission field** to you!"

- Brother Andrew, God's Smuggler

OPERATION WORLD DAY

Your college campus needs Jesus, but so does the entire world. God's concern is not only for your campus, hometown, state, or country—He cares about the entire world, and has called us to have the same compassion. He has called us to go and make disciples of all nations.

Here are some practical ways to participate in Operation World Day!

1. Reach out to as many students from other countries as you can today, just to get to know them and to learn about where they are from at first.

2. Pray for a missionary or a country. Think of practical needs and seek to meet one if it is possible.

3. Pray that more people would go abroad as missionaries—and ask God   if He would have you to go.

4. Ask God if it is His will for you to go on a short-term mission this summer.

5. "The Justice Revolution" is another book that focuses entirely on injustice around the world, and on what you can do to pray and help. It will radically affect your life. You can order it on www.operationlightforce.com—and you may change not just your school, but also the whole world.

SOCIAL MEDIA ASSIGNMENT - Post the following verse or share site about missions, a short-term mission opportunity or something you learned about missions today.

> **Matthew 28:19** *"Therefore, go and make disciples of all nations, baptizing them in the name of the Father and of the Son and of the Holy Spirit, and teaching them to obey everything I have commanded you. And surely I am with you always, to the very end of the age."*

EXTREME DAYS
A STRATEGY FOR AN AWAKENING ON YOUR CAMPUS

ADAPTED FROM
40 DAY REVOLUTION

JOURNAL

How has the world come to me? What can I do to intentionally impact the world from where God has me right now?

_____

_____

_____

_____

_____

_____

REVOLUTIONARY QUOTE

"The kingdom of God is a new order founded on the fatherly love of God, on redemption, justice and fellowship. It is meant to enter into all life, all nations, and all policies until the kingdom of this world becomes the kingdom of the Lord."

—ERIC LIDDELL, OLYMPIC GOLD-MEDAL WINNER AND MISSIONARY TO CHINA

PRAYER

Pray today for the people around you who come from all around the world. Also, pray today for missionaries and those who are taking the gospel into the entire world.

_____

_____

_____

_____

_____

_____

WEEK 5 ~ MEMORY VERSE:

II Corinthians 10:4,5, KJV—Prayer Evangelism

"For the weapons of our warfare are not carnal, but mighty through God to the pulling down of strong holds; casting down imaginations, and every high thing that exalteth itself against the knowledge of God, and bringing into captivity every thought to the obedience of Christ."

Too many Christians have spent their entire Christian lives living as slaves to sin and the enemy, even though Christ has already purchased their freedom. Christ came that you might have life, and have it more abundantly.

THE PURGE DAY

Look at the list below and make a list of any involvement you have ever had in any of theses areas, then ask forgiveness, and renounce all involvement according to God's leading. It is best to write out the specifics as He reveals them to you, confess, ask His forgiveness, renounce all, and receive God's forgiveness—and then burn the list.

1. **Unforgiveness**: List all of the people from childhood to the present toward whom you have ever had any unforgiveness or resentment.

2. **The Occult:** Séances, Santeria, Dungeons and Dragons, Ouija boards, tarot cards, palm reading, psychics, witchcraft, and others.

3. **Sexual Sin:** premarital sex, lust, masturbation, adultery, pornography, homosexuality, lesbianism, rape, molestation.

4. **Soul Ties:** People that have had an ungodly control over you.

5. **Covenants, Vows, and Curses**: List all broken vows.

6. **Abuses:** verbal, emotional, sexual, psychological, or even spiritual hurts and rejections, both those received and those given.

7. **Death:** List deceased family members whose evil traits or character qualities have been attributed to you.

8. **Cursed objects and buildings:** List places of evil you have visited.

9. **Fears and Phobias:** List fears or phobias that are areas of struggle.

10. **Addictions:** List substances, foods, or behaviors that you find addictive.

SOCIAL MEDIA ASSIGNMENT - Purge yourself of any friends within your social media who post inappropriate things or don't honor God. You can unfollow people on Facebook without deleting them as friends; so they can still see what you post, but you cant see what they post.

> **1 Thessalonians 5:23** "May God himself, the God of peace, sanctify you through and through. May your whole spirit, soul and body be kept blameless at the coming of our Lord Jesus Christ."

> **Daniel 4:27** "...Renounce your sins by doing right, and your wickedness by being kind to the oppressed. It may be that then your prosperity will continue."

> **I John 5:4** "for everyone born of God overcomes the world. This is the victory that has overcome the world, even our faith."

JOURNAL

Today your entire assignment involves journaling and purging your life of those things God wants to clean out.

_____

_____

_____

_____

_____

_____

_____

REVOLUTIONARY QUOTE

"The battle for the soul of this generation will not be won by a show of brute force. True conversion does not come by the sword but by the cross; not by taking of life but by the laying down of life."

—MICHAEL BROWN, AUTHOR OF REVOLUTION

PRAYER

Today spend the time journaling and praying for God's forgiveness and cleansing of your life so that you can be the missionary God has called you to be.

_____

_____

_____

_____

_____

_____

WEEK 5 ~ MEMORY VERSE:

II Corinthians 10:4,5, KJV—Prayer Evangelism

"For the weapons of our warfare are not carnal, but mighty through God to the pulling down of strong holds; casting down imaginations, and every high thing that exalteth itself against the knowledge of God, and bringing into captivity every thought to the obedience of Christ."

Suicide is the second-leading cause of death among people aged 25 to 34 and the third-leading cause of death among people aged 15 to 24. There are more than 1,000 suicides on college campuses per year.

LIFE DAY

It's so bad in fact, that 1 in 10 college students have made a plan for suicide. This is something that needs to stop. Most of these people feel as though there is no one who cares for them and no one would miss them. They need to be told about what Jesus did for them and that there are people who care about them.

1. Today pray against a spirit of death and suicide at your school. Take at least 30 minutes to intercede for the students at your campus who feel like no one cares for them.

2. Be the light! Let the Holy Spirit lead you and open your eyes today to anyone and everyone who needs encouragement and love today. You never know what your actions could change.

3. Talk with your friends, you would be surprised at how many of them have had suicidal thoughts.

4. If this is an area you have ever struggled with, break any and all agreements you have ever made with death. Tell your pastor and ask him to pray with you and help you.

SOCIAL MEDIA ASSIGNMENT - Post something about people 25 through 34 and how suicides are the second leading cause of death of people 15 to 24 but also say there is always hope in Jesus. Make yourself available to anyone who has or is struggling in this area.

> *1 Corinthians 15:55-57 (KJV)* "O death, where is your sting? O grave, where is your victory? The sting of death is sin; and the strength of sin is the law. But thanks [be] to God, which gives us the victory through our Lord Jesus Christ."

JOURNAL

Ask God to show you anyone who is struggling with thoughts of Suicide? Ask the Lord what He would have you do?

_____

_____

_____

_____

_____

_____

REVOLUTIONARY QUOTE

"Life is either a daring adventure or nothing. Security does not exist in nature, nor do the children of men as a whole experience it. Avoiding danger is no safer in the long run than exposure."

—HELLEN KELLER

PRAYER

Ask God for freedom if you have ever asked God to kill you, wished you were dead, thought of or attempted suicide. Pray against a spirit of death and for those God shows to you who may be dealing with thoughts of suicide.

_____

_____

_____

_____

_____

_____

WEEK 5 ~ MEMORY VERSE:

II Corinthians 10:4,5, KJV—Prayer Evangelism

"For the weapons of our warfare are not carnal, but mighty through God to the pulling down of strong holds; casting down imaginations, and every high thing that exalteth itself against the knowledge of God, and bringing into captivity every thought to the obedience of Christ."

"It has been said that for evil men to accomplish their purpose it is only necessary that good men should do nothing." ~ ***Rev. Charles F. Aked***

TAKE A STAND DAY

Today stand up for what you believe! Jesus took a stand in the temple. I'm not telling you to flip your desk, and yell, "Enough!" This is a follow up to Giants day. You have been praying about these giants in your school for 30 days, and today you take your stand.

In Luke 10:19, Jesus tells the 72 others that he has given them authority to trample snakes and scorpions, and to overcome all the power of the enemy—and that's exactly what you're going to do.

What do you do when you hear someone curse or use God's name in vain? What do you do when you hear someone talking behind a teachers back, or slandering a classmate? Do you ever take a stand against anything? It has become unpopular in our society to come against anything except intolerance.

We don't wrestle against flesh and blood but against principalities and spiritual forces. It is time to pray against the forces of darkness on our campus and to speak up. Reach out in love to your friends and compel them not to drink, do drugs, lie, cheat or swear. Understand that you may face persecution for what you say and do, but the Bible says to count it as pure joy when you face persecution for Christ's name! Matthew 5:11-12

1. When your friends do something you know is not right, don't let it slide. Take a stand—but be careful to do it in LOVE!!!!

2. If anything came to mind that you knew was wrong, but you didn't say anything repent and ask God what you should do.

3. Pray that your eyes will be open to the schemes of the enemy at work in your school, and ask God how you can stop them!

SOCIAL MEDIA ASSIGNMENT - Take a stand on your social media in a loving way. Don't get in arguments, but in a loving way confront things that aren't glorifying to the Lord. Send private messages instead of commenting for the whole world to see. Also post this verse

> ***James 5:20*** *"Remember this: Whoever turns a sinner from the error of their way will save them from death and cover over a multitude of sins."*

EXTREME DAYS
A STRATEGY FOR AN AWAKENING ON YOUR CAMPUS

ADAPTED FROM
40 DAY
REVOLUTION

JOURNAL

What changes could happen in your school if someone or a group took a stand?

_____

_____

_____

_____

_____

_____

REVOLUTIONARY QUOTE

"The sin of silence when they should protest makes cowards of men."

—ABRAHAM LINCOLN

PRAYER

Ask God to show you those things that need to be confronted at your school and pray for courage in yourself and others to take a stand.

_____

_____

_____

_____

_____

_____

WEEK 5 ~ MEMORY VERSE:

II Corinthians 10:4,5, KJV—Prayer Evangelism

"For the weapons of our warfare are not carnal, but mighty through God to the pulling down of strong holds; casting down imaginations, and every high thing that exalteth itself against the knowledge of God, and bringing into captivity every thought to the obedience of Christ."

HOME PRAYER WALK DAY

The place in which you spend most of your time (even if a lot of it is asleep) is in your home. Just as Joshua made the declaration, "As for me and my house we will serve the Lord." You must dedicate your home to the Lord. Maybe you have an apartment, live at home, or live in dorms, wherever you live is your home.

1. Pray in every room of your house, dorm, or apartment. Pray that each room will be full of the peace and presence of the Lord.

2. Pray that your home is hospitable and useful for leading people to Christ.

3. If your family, friends, roommates, or floor mates will join you, pray with your friends at each other's homes.

4. Walk the perimeter of your property praying over the land, and declaring that the land belongs to the Lord. Also, repent of any sins that have happened on the land, and pray that God would restore the land.

SOCIAL MEDIA ASSIGNMENT - Post this verse.

Joshua 24:15 (NKJV) *"And if it seems evil to you to serve the LORD, choose for yourselves this day whom you will serve, whether the gods which your fathers served that [were] on the other side of the River, or the gods of the Amorites, in whose land you dwell. But as for me and my house, we will serve the LORD."*

EXTREME DAYS
A STRATEGY FOR AN AWAKENING ON YOUR CAMPUS

ADAPTED FROM
40 DAY
REVOLUTION

JOURNAL

Ask the Lord, how He wants you to use your dorm, apartment or house for Him.

_____

_____

_____

_____

_____

QUOTE

"When the Spiritual climate changes for the better, so does everybody and everything in the city {home, dorm, apartment building}."

—ED SILVOSO, AUTHOR OF THAT NONE SHOULD PERISH & PRAYER EVANGELISM

PRAYER

You will be praying throughout your room, apartment, or home. Pray for more opportunities to minister and for the Holy Spirit to fill your home.

_____

_____

_____

_____

_____

WEEK 5 ~ MEMORY VERSE:

II Corinthians 10:4,5, KJV—Prayer Evangelism

"For the weapons of our warfare are not carnal, but mighty through God to the pulling down of strong holds; casting down imaginations, and every high thing that exalteth itself against the knowledge of God, and bringing into captivity every thought to the obedience of Christ."

LIGHTHOUSE DAY V - BLESS THE PASTOR DAY

Your pastors have a great responsibility for the souls of your church. God has surely used one or more pastors in your life to speak to you. Even God's Word encourages us to honor those who have blessed us. Today make an extra special effort to bless your pastor(s) and/ or youth pastor.

Hopefully while your going to college your plugged into a local church. Where you have a place of encouragement and refuge from the crazy college life. If not, then go find one.

1. Ask your pastor if there is anything you can do to serve him or her, or the church.

2. Write him or her an encouraging note.

3. Give him or her a gift.

4. Be an active member of the body of Christ.

5. Say something encouraging to him or her.

6. Give him or her a hug.

SOCIAL MEDIA ASSIGNMENT - Write something that will bless your pastor.

Also since today is a "Lighthouse Day," seek to meet or speak to two new neighbors whom you've not yet reached out to, and minister to their needs. Add their needs to your Lighthouse Prayer Guide.

> *I Corinthians 12:25-26* "So that there should be no division in the body, but that its parts should have equal concern for each other. If one part suffers, every part suffers with it; if one part is honored, every part rejoices with it."

A STRATEGY FOR AN AWAKENING ON YOUR CAMPUS

ADAPTED FROM

JOURNAL

What has your pastor(s) done to impact your life in a positive ways? What are the things about your pastor(s) that remind you of Jesus?

_____

_____

_____

_____

_____

_____

REVOLUTIONARY QUOTE

"There is no such thing as a self-made spiritual leader. A true leader influences others spiritually only because the Spirit works in and through him to a greater degree than in those he leads." — J. OSWALD SANDERS

PRAYER

Pray for your spiritual leaders today. Pray for blessing over their marriage, relationships, finances, and most importantly their walk with God.

_____

_____

_____

_____

_____

_____

WEEK 6 ~ MEMORY VERSE:

II Timothy 1:13-14

"What you have heard from me, keep as the pattern of sound teaching, with faith and love in Christ Jesus. Guard the good deposit that was entrusted to you—guard it with the help of the Holy Spirit who lives in us."

[ASSIGNMENT] WEEK 6 ~ DAY 37 ~ MONDAY ___/___/___
[TODAY'S DATE]

School clubs are an important arena of interaction that can be used for God's purpose. Whether you are in a Christian club or any other type of club, you need to realize that you are to be a revolutionary for Jesus. Don't be molded into the norm. Set the standard!

CAMPUS CLUB DAY

Small groups, accountability groups, support groups and similar groups are a vital part of God's purpose. You should be faithfully meeting at a point each week, not only during these 40 days but all year long. Jesus Himself made the focus of His ministry 12 men. It is imperative that you plug into a small group. Today, if you are already in a small group find a way to bless your small group, its leaders and other members. If you are not involved in one then make an effort to join or begin a small group.

Romans 12:2 (NIV) teaches us, *"Do not conform to the pattern of this world, but be transformed by the renewing of your mind. Then you will be able to test and approve what God's will is—his good, pleasing and perfect will."*

Today, find a way to bless your club, its leaders, and other members.

1. Pray for the leaders and sponsors of campus clubs. Pray for God's will to be done.

2. Attend the next meeting or start a campus club (i.e., Fellowship of Christian Athletes, Student Venture, Youth for Christ, or Young Life).

3. Some students have blessed clubs that Christians normally shun, like the gay club or some other club. Serving those whom others shun can open the door for powerful witnessing.

4. Start a Bible study with someone. Faith, commitment, and accountability found in meeting with others on campus are critical for your spiritual growth.

   Matthew 9:37~10:1 *"The harvest is plentiful but the workers are few. Ask the Lord of the harvest, therefore, to send out workers into His harvest field. He called His 12 disciples to Him and gave them authority to drive out evil spirits and to heal every disease and sickness."*

SOCIAL MEDIA ASSIGNMENT - Post this verse:

1 Peter 2:2 *"Like newborn babies, crave pure spiritual milk, so that by it you may grow up in salvation."*

JOURNAL

How have I been impacted by a small group of believers in my life? What could I do to impact others more in the same way?

_____

_____

_____

_____

_____

QUOTE

"Jesus called his 12 disciples, knowing that the harvest was too plentiful for one person to reap it. He needed to work through others to minister to the masses."

— JOEL COMISKEY, AUTHOR OF G12 GROUPS

PRAYER

Pray for the people in your small group if you have one. If you don't have a small group or a Christian club, ask the Lord who you could begin to meet with to encourage, pray for one another and serve one another.

_____

_____

_____

_____

_____

_____

WEEK 6 ~ MEMORY VERSE:

II Timothy 1:13-14

"What you have heard from me, keep as the pattern of sound teaching, with faith and love in Christ Jesus. Guard the good deposit that was entrusted to you—guard it with the help of the Holy Spirit who lives in us."

There are men and women, who are working on campus all day and you likely have hardly ever noticed them. You have the librarians, food servers, grounds and maintenance people, or the janitor. They are too often not appreciated or acknowledged. Make their day by showing appreciation.

UNSUNG HERO/CUSTODIAN DAY

You may decide to reach out to one person, or to several. You never know what a word of encouragement will mean to someone. People serve you every day without receiving even a word of appreciation. At least today, let's change our approach and become more grateful. Better yet, make it a habit.

1. Ask if there is any way you can pray for them and then—if they will let you—pray for them.

2. Write a note to someone to let him or her know that he or she is special . . . and you prayed for him or her today.

3. Give them a small gift of appreciation, a drink, candy bar, or something nicer.

4. Buy one or more of them lunch.

Ephesians 4:29 "Do not let any unwholesome talk come out of your mouths, but only what is helpful for building others up according to their needs, that it may benefit those who listen."

SOCIAL MEDIA ASSIGNMENT - Post something that shows appreciation for an unsung hero today and tag them in it. Encourage others to reach out

JOURNAL

Which unsung heroes can I bless/serve/pray for or communicate with today? ?

_____

_____

_____

_____

_____

_____

QUOTE

"This experience of ours is really worth taking a couple of bullets for. [If you do come,] don't think of returning, the revolution won't wait."

—CHE GUEVARA, INVITING HIS OLD FRIEND JULIO "EL GUACHO" CASTRO TO JOIN HIM IN CUBA

PRAYER

Pray for God to open your eyes to the people who serve without much recognition. Pray for their needs today.

_____

_____

_____

_____

WEEK 6 ~ MEMORY VERSE:

II Timothy 1:13-14

"What you have heard from me, keep as the pattern of sound teaching, with faith and love in Christ Jesus. Guard the good deposit that was entrusted to you— guard it with the help of the Holy Spirit who lives in us."

Fasting anything can help us break addictions and also get a new perspective. Today you will fast all forms of media except what you have to for work or school.

MEDIA FAST DAY

Wow, we use media a lot! It seems to have taken over our lives. If we spend more time watching TV, on the computer or on our phone then we do with God whom are we really serving? Today is the day to be free from every form of media, except for the Bible and your homework. In 2013, college students spent 60% of their day interacting with technology – 14.4 hours daily. Roughly 5 hours on their laptops, 3.5 on their phones, and nearly 3 hours watching TV.

___ TV and videos	___ Radio	___ Newspaper	
___ Audio CDs	___ Internet	___ Movies	___ Cell Phone
___ Facebook	___ Twitter	___ Snapchat	___ Instagram
___ Texting	___ IPods	___ Computer	

Devote the time you save to reading the Bible and praying. (**See Daniel 1:8-20.**)

> **Psalm 101:2-3** *"I will be careful to lead a blameless life—when will you come to me? I will walk in my house with blameless heart. I will set before my eyes no vile thing."*

SOCIAL MEDIA ASSIGNMENT - DO NOTHING! Make a commitment to honor God in all of your media use.

EXTREME DAYS
A STRATEGY FOR AN AWAKENING ON YOUR CAMPUS
ADAPTED FROM
40 DAY REVOLUTION

JOURNAL

What is the hardest media for me to fast and why? How did fasting media impact me? How long can I go without any form of media? Why? How much influence does media have on my life? For good? For bad?

_____

_____

_____

_____

_____

REVOLUTIONARY QUOTE

"Prayer is the most unexplored area of the Christian life.
Prayer is the most powerful weapon of the Christian life.
Prayer is the most hell-feared battle in the Christian life.
Prayer is the most secret device of the Christian life.
Prayer is the most underestimated power in the Christian life.
Prayer is the most untaught truth in the Christian life.
Prayer is the most demanding exercise in the Christian life.
Prayer is the most neglected responsibility in the Christian life.
Prayer is the most conquering outreach in the Christian life.
Prayer is the most opposed warfare in the Christian life.
Prayer is the most far-reaching ministry in the Christian life."
—LEONARD RAVENHILL, AUTHOR AND EVANGELIST

PRAYER

Spend time today asking God to be Lord of your life in regards to all forms of media. You will have a lot of extra time today, use it wisely and devote extra time to praying.

_____

_____

_____

WEEK 6 ~ MEMORY VERSE:

II Timothy 1:13-14

"What you have heard from me, keep as the pattern of sound teaching, with faith and love in Christ Jesus. Guard the good deposit that was entrusted to you— guard it with the help of the Holy Spirit who lives in us."

If you are reading this and you have managed to keep your commitment to carry out all or many of the 40-Day Revolution assignments then you deserve a round of applause. You have made a tremendous impact on the world around you whether you realize it or not. You have stepped outside your comfort zone and done something that most people wouldn't be willing to do. Congratulations..

IT IS FINISHED!

You may have finished the 40-Day Revolution, but it is really just the start. Think about what will last eternally because of your involvement in the 40-Day Revolution. The goal of this has been both to change the spiritual climate of the world around you as well as to develop a lifestyle in you of reaching out and impacting your world.

1. You know the stickers you wear after you vote? Well today you are encouraged to make an "It is Finished" sticker, on your computer or by hand, and then wear it!

   a. Explain to people that you are finishing the 40-day fast

   b. Explain that when Jesus died, He said, "It is finished" which means "paid in full."

   c. Explain that He paid for our sins. Finish strong, just like Jesus did.

2. Your campaign fast is completed at the end of the day. Celebrate with some friends. If you want, eat or drink whatever you've been fasting, and share stories of your experiences.

3. Your spiritual journey is just beginning! Think about and talk about how to keep the revolution alive.

4. Sit down and make a list of the things you have seen God do over the last 40 days.

5. E-mail your testimonies to: operationlightforce@gmail.com.

SOCIAL MEDIA ASSIGNMENT - Tell the world about what God has done in your life during the last 40 days

> *John 19:30* *"When he had received the drink, Jesus said, 'It is finished.' With that, he bowed his head and gave up his spirit."*

JOURNAL

How has God changed my life? My college group? My campus?

_____
_____
_____
_____
_____
_____
_____
_____
_____
_____
_____

PRAYER

Ask God to help you apply what you have learned. Ask God for his direction and strength regarding adjusting your lifestyle so that you can continue to bear much fruit.

_____
_____
_____
_____
_____
_____
_____

WEEK 6 ~ MEMORY VERSE:

II Timothy 1:13-14

"What you have heard from me, keep as the pattern of sound teaching, with faith and love in Christ Jesus. Guard the good deposit that was entrusted to you—guard it with the help of the Holy Spirit who lives in us."

[CONGRATULATIONS!]

You have just completed a **40-day assault** on the enemy's spiritual forces in your home and at school. For persevering to the end, you deserve a **"Medal of Honor."** You have become engaged in a revolution that will not stop until **Christ Jesus** returns.

KNOW THIS

You have impacted the spiritual climate of your campus, your family members, and the lives of other students in significant ways for Christ. You have made a mess of Satan's strategies, advanced Christ's kingdom, matured spiritually, and you have developed some habits that we pray will last for a lifetime.

REMEMBER

The battle is not over. Your mission has only begun. Now, your mission, should you choose to accept it, is this:

1. Love others in practical and tangible ways.

2. Serve others even as Christ served us and gave His life for us while we were still sinners.

3. Speak words of blessings to all of your friends, peers, and, yes, even your enemies.

4. Pray for the unsaved harvest. Pray for their healing, their relationship to God, and their well-being.

5. Keep on telling people about the love of God, and His gift of eternal life through Jesus' death and resurrection. Tell them how they can know God.

EXTREME DAYS

A STRATEGY FOR AN AWAKENING ON YOUR CAMPUS

ADAPTED FROM:

(APPENDICES)

[FORGIVENESS]

Jesus taught us **forgiveness** by His words and by His actions. In **Matthew 6,** when Jesus taught the disciples how to pray He said, ***"Forgive us…as we forgive others."*** It is the only part of the prayer that Jesus went on to explain to the disciples more fully.

Jesus said to His disciples that if we don't forgive others, then our heavenly Father won't forgive us. We all desperately need God's forgiveness. All of us have sinned. God wants you to be free from shame, condemnation and guilt. He sent His only Son Jesus to pay the penalty that you and I deserved to pay, so that we can be totally forgiven and cleansed.

One of the only prerequisites for being forgiven and receiving His forgiveness is to forgive others. I know that you have been hurt deeply by someone in your life. Some of you have had a life full of deep hurts, wounds, betrayal and abuse. It seems impossible to forgive those who hurt you. Their words or actions may have devastated you. For some it is your father or mother whom you loved but who walked out on you. For some it is the person who broke your trust or violated you.

It isn't easy, but it is vital for your own well-being, for your relationship with God, and for your future well being that you forgive anyone and everyone.

Let me clarify here what I am not saying.

First of all, I am not saying that if you are currently in an abusive relationship that you need to do nothing and allow the abuse to continue. If the situation warrants it, you can call the authorities, and have the person arrested. Even then, you will still need to forgive that person if you want to live a healthy life, know peace and joy in your heart.

Second, I'm not saying that you have to be best friends with those who have hurt you. You can forgive someone and maintain a healthy distance from them.

If the person who has hurt you the most is a family member and you are still around that person every day, you may need to do more than just forgive them one time. The forgiveness will be an ongoing process, and you may need to share with them many times how what they are saying or doing affects you, hurts you, and what you would prefer.

In Matthew 18, Peter asked the Lord how many times he should forgive his brother who sins against him, "7 times?" Jesus replied, no Peter, 7 times 70 times. He then told a story of a man who was forgiven a vast debt and then couldn't forgive someone who owed him. Jesus concludes that if we don't forgive others we will be tormented. Unforgiveness brings torment to our soul, our mind and to our body.

Take the time to examine your life and write down the names of everyone who has hurt you. Ask God to forgive them, ask God to help you to forgive them, then forgive that person—and do it as often as you need to.

If forgiveness is hard for you because people have hurt you deeply get more teaching on forgiveness at:

http://operationlightforce.com/100-foundational/352-jesse-s-testimony-21

[CATALOGUE]

www.40dayrevolution.com

Resources to help youth leaders carry out an effective revolution.

40-Day Revolution App

REVOLUTION OUT OF THE BOX!

If you're looking for a strategy that will help you equip your students to take their schools back for Christ . . . look no further. We understand what it takes to be a youth pastor and to work with a limited budget. That's one of the reasons we've developed Revolution Out of the Box. This exciting, new curriculum is now available!

Revolution Out of the Box contains virtually everything you need to launch a revolution! It includes: six completely prepared, powerful lessons, small group questions and handouts, video clips, Bible studies, and The 40-Day Revolution book with supply packet. Everything you need to help your students sustain a revolution for an entire six weeks!

Call Operation Light Force or go to the merchandise section on our website and check it out! Order your Revolution Out of the Box today!

- Two powerful videos to motivate, inspire, and challenge.

- Leader's Training Manual, which includes six powerful, complete lessons to help you cast the vision and train your students.

- A Supply Packet including The 40-Day Revolution book, tracts, notecards, dog tag, assignment cards.

JESUS TRAINING MANUAL

Jesus commanded His followers to "go and make disciples of all nations." This book dares you to examine how Jesus Himself made disciples.

Richard Mull's honest account of his personal journey toward biblical discipleship presents a dilemma for twenty-first-century believers: Will we adopt a system of belief that explains why we disciple differently than Jesus did, or must we admit that in spite of our education and experience, we may not be making disciples according to Jesus' teaching?

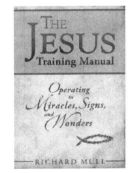

God desires to take you on a journey much like that of Jesus' first disciples, who learned to do what Jesus was doing by observing Him in action and obeying what He taught. Lord, Disciple Me will challenge you to develop a biblical foundation for your journey. Jesus will provide the hands-on experience!!

[CATALOGUE]

"40 DAYS TO TRANSFORMATION MANUAL"

Written for and geared toward adults, this manual will guide you on a 40-day "mission" to bring about spiritual transformation in your life, workplace, home, neighborhood, and even your city! You will learn what "transformation" really is, as well as a comprehensive understanding about what it means to fast and see God's power released through blessing, servant, and prayer evangelism.

"AGAPE REVOLUTION"

Children have been excited by what they've seen take place in their older brothers and sisters—now they can be a part, too! This manual puts simple tools into their hands that will help them change their world for Jesus. Each book contains an explanation of each of the 40 assignments, as well as quotes, scriptures, and challenges that will keep children motivated and focused during the 40 days.

"THE 40-DAY CAMPUS REVOLUTION" MANUAL

College campuses have been the starting points of most of the revolutions launched around the world—why should it be any different for this kind of "counterculture" revolution? Each manual gives a great understanding of what it means to fast and pray, the elements of the revolution, and a complete explanation about each of the 40 assignments that will be carried out over the 40 days.

ONE DAY TRAINING CONFERENCE

We will bring a one-day, four-hour training session to your city to assist you in launching "The 40-Days" with your youth group, or better yet, with your entire church family! We will focus on training and equipping each participant to understand the power of prayer, servant and blessing evangelism, and fasting.

We have seen a near 100% commitment by those who attend a ONE DAY Training to carry out the 40 days' assignments. Lives, schools, cities, neighborhoods, workplaces, and homes are radically changed for God's kingdom. Why wait? Schedule a conference and prepare to "launch a revolution" today!

LORD HEAL ME

"Lord, Heal Me" Traces the biblical foundation of healing from Genesis to Revelation. There are many testimonies of God healing the sick today. You will grow in faith and in understanding of what the bible teaches about this very important subject. This is a must for every follower of Jesus who wants to be like Jesus, do what Jesus did and teach what Jesus taught.

GOD SPEAKS BIBLE

An amazing Bible that will help you to live the supernatural life. It will impact Bible reading for a new generation. This Bible highlights every time that God speaks throughout the Bible. It also highlights every miracle and every dream, vision and encounter with angels.

OPERATION LIGHT FORCE
2310 Leonard Drive | Seffner, FL 33584
www.operationlightforce.com
www.40dayrevolution.com
813.657.6147 phone

Made in United States
Orlando, FL
15 September 2022